Higher Education and School Reform

P. Michael Timpane

Lori S. White

Editors

Higher Education
and
School Reform

Jossey-Bass Publishers • San Francisco

Jossey-Bass books and products are available through most
bookstores. To contact Jossey-Bass directly, call (888) 378–2537,
fax to (800) 605–2665, or visit our website at www.josseybass.com.

Substantial discounts on bulk quantities of Jossey-Bass books are
available to corporations, professional associations, and other
organizations. For details and discount information, contact the
special sales department at Jossey-Bass.

For sales outside the United States, please contact your local Simon
& Schuster International Office.

 Manufactured in the United States of America on Lyons Falls
Turin Book. This paper is acid-free and 100 percent totally
chlorine-free.

Library of Congress Cataloging-in-Publication Data
Higher education and school reform / P. Michael Timpane,
     Lori S.White, editors. — 1st ed.
          p. cm. — (Jossey-Bass education series) (Jossey-Bass higher
          and adult education series)
     Includes index.
     ISBN 0–7879–4062–3 (cloth : acid-free paper)
     1. Education, Higher—United States—Administration.
2. Educational change—United States. 3. College-school
cooperation—United States. 4. Higher education and state—
United States. I. Timpane, P. Michael, date II. White, Lori S., date
III. Series. IV. Series: Jossey-Bass higher and adult education series
LB2341 .H523 1998
378.73—ddc21   98–8976

FIRST EDITION
HB Printing   10 9 8 7 6 5 4 3 2 1

A joint publication in

The Jossey-Bass Education Series

and

The Jossey-Bass Higher and

Adult Education Series

Contents

Preface

In the course of the diverse school reform initiatives launched in the 1980s and 1990s, little attention has been paid to the role of higher education, either by school reformers or by higher education leaders. Although particular aspects of school–higher education relationships (teacher education most prominently) are addressed in the school reform literature, there is no work that provides a comprehensive review of the relationship of higher education and schools, particularly within the framework of systemic education reform.[1]

School reform efforts are in particular need of the help that higher education can provide, both that traditionally provided (well-trained professionals; research and development products) and new help in the form of partnerships, policy advocacy and support, clear guidance on academic standards and requirements, and coordinated policy development and political action.

Additionally, higher education is increasingly subject to calls for reform along lines similar to those proposed for reforming schools: goals and standards, outcomes and assessment, organizational restructuring and incentives, and greater attention to teaching and learning. Some would argue that these sorts of reforms are greatly needed in higher education; others that they are wholly improbable or inappropriate.

The Pew Forum on Education Reform is a group of policymakers, higher education faculty, school administrators, teachers, and community leaders who gathered three or four times a year from 1990 to 1996 to examine issues of systemic education reform.

Broadly defined, systemic education reform is the alignment of state and national policy systems to support sustained efforts for local school reform to provide high-quality curriculum and instruction to students.[2] Noting the absence of significant higher education involvement in policy-level discussions on school reform, the Forum commissioned this volume to stimulate discussion and debate on how higher education and schools are or should be working together for the improvement of schools and, consequently, colleges and universities.

This volume seeks to add to current knowledge and practice by helping to define how schools and higher education relate to and depend upon each other and by examining, in particular, the extent to which higher education can and should respond to meet the assumptions of systemic education reform in the schools.

Specifically, this book seeks to

- Provide a historical and contemporary perspective on the nature of the relationships between higher education and schools and discuss why, whether, and to what extent higher education should be involved in school reform

- Analyze in greater depth particular aspects of higher education–school interactions—teacher education, partnerships for learning, curricular articulations, and faculty experiences—and comment on the structural and philosophical realities that inhibit changes in the scope, depth, and effectiveness of these interactions

- Explore new conceptualizations of the relationship between higher education and schools, and suggest the impact of such models on higher education policy and practice

We try to step back from the issues as they often arise. We talk in little detail about some of the traditionally studied relationships between higher education and schools, such as teacher preparation in schools of education or college admissions practices. We touch only briefly on the issues of student financial assistance, even though they may be more important than academic concerns in determining the extent of access and goodness of fit between matriculating students and the specific institutions they attend. We devote one chapter to a review of the promise and progress of school-college-community partnerships, but deliberately say little else about the school side of the relationship in the belief that a focus on the higher education side will do more to advance the discussion at this time. We focus primarily on four-year postsecondary institutions rather than on two-year colleges (where the need and potential for stronger ties with schools are equally great but greatly constrained by the policies and practices of colleges and universities).

Instead, we examine a set of issues that underlie the difficulties encountered in making substantial progress in these familiar, important, and exceedingly durable domains: namely, the continuing impact of encrusted historical differences and disparities between higher education and schools, as well as contemporary divisions of governance; the likely extent to which university faculty can or will change their behaviors in ways reformers assume they must; the appropriate conceptual bases for the conduct of teacher education in universities and for the reconstruction of shared academic purposes between schools and higher education; and the extent to which our nation's way of thinking about and organizing its educational enterprise creates issues scarcely recognized in other lands. We contend that in these domains lie many of the pitfalls and snares that frustrate our progress on the more visible terrain of policy and practice, and that we must address such basic issues of value, belief, and incentive if we expect to understand or change behavior and create circumstances in which schools and colleges work together extensively to their mutual benefit.

Acknowledgments

This volume is the culmination of three years of stimulating conversations with the contributing authors and others interested in exploring higher education's role in school reform. The editors would like to thank the Pew Forum on Education Reform, Milbrey McLaughlin, and Robert Schwartz in particular, and our respective colleagues at RAND, the Carnegie Foundation for the Advancement of Teaching, and Stanford University for their support in producing this volume.

March 1998   P. Michael Timpane
                                                    Washington, D.C.

                                                    Lori S. White
                                                    Stanford, California

Notes

1. Sirotnik (1988) and Clark (1985) are two books that look at particular aspects of the relationship between higher education and schools. Sirotnik's book focuses primarily on the relationships between schools and universities with respect to teacher training and university faculty research on school practices; the Clark book is a cross-national comparison of the relationship between higher education and schools in selected countries.
2. See O'Day and Smith (1993).

References

Clark, B. *The School and the University*. Berkeley: University of California Press, 1985.

O'Day, J. A., and Smith, M. S. "Systemic Reform and Educational Opportunity." In S. H. Fuhrman (ed.), *Designing Coherent Education Policy: Improving the System*. San Francisco: Jossey-Bass, 1993.

Sirotnik, K. A. (ed.). *School-University Partnerships in Action: Concepts, Cases and Concerns*. New York: Teachers College Press, 1988.

The Editors

P. Michael Timpane is a senior advisor for education policy for RAND and has served as vice president and senior scholar at the Carnegie Foundation for the Advancement of Teaching. He is also professor of education and former president, Teachers College, Columbia University. He has conducted research on educational policy as a senior staff member at the Brookings Institution and the RAND Corporation, and served before that as director of education policy planning for the Department of Health, Education, and Welfare. Timpane has published numerous articles on educational policy and has edited and contributed to several books on education and social policy. For over two decades he has helped direct the Aspen Institutes Program for Education in a Changing Society. Through this, and as advisor to state and federal policymakers, Timpane has been involved in the development of national goals and standards in education; new formulations of policy with respect to comprehensive services for young children, higher education, education, and work; learning and technology; and national education reform. Timpane received a B.A. degree in history and economics *magna cum laude* from Catholic University in 1956, an M.A. degree in history from the same institution, and an M.P.A. from Harvard University. He has received honorary doctorates from Wagner College and Catholic University.

Lori S. White is assistant vice-provost for undergraduate education at Stanford University and a lecturer in the Stanford University

School of Education. She has worked in higher education administration for over sixteen years at the University of California and at Georgetown and Stanford Universities. Prior to assuming her current position, she was the director of student programs at Georgetown University. She has also worked as director of the Cross Cultural Center and as assistant dean of students at the University of California, Irvine. In addition, her work in higher education has included serving as a committee consultant to the California State Assembly Committee on Higher Education and as a special assistant to the University of California, office of the president. She has also worked in the K–12 policy arena as a special assistant to the San Francisco superintendent of schools and as a research assistant to the Pew Forum on Education Reform. White received her B.A. in English and psychology from the University of California, Berkeley, and her Ph.D. in education policy from Stanford University.

The Contributors

Patrick M. Callan is executive director of the California Higher Education Policy Center. The Center is an independent, nonpartisan, nonprofit organization founded in 1992 to stimulate examination and public discussion of the future of California higher education. Callan's primary focus is education policy. He has served as vice president of the Education Commission of the States, executive director of the California Postsecondary Education Commission, executive director of the Washington State Council on Postsecondary Education, and as executive director of the Montana Commission on Postsecondary Education. He has been a member of numerous national, regional, and state commissions and has written and spoken extensively on education and public policy. He has been an advisor to blue ribbon commissions, state education and higher education boards, governor's offices, and legislative committees in more than half the states and a consultant and project leader for the Chinese Provincial Universities Development Project sponsored by the World Bank.

David K. Cohen is John Dewey Collegiate Professor of Education and professor of public policy at the University of Michigan. Prior to his appointment to the University of Michigan, he was John A. Hannah Distinguished Professor of Education and Social Policy at Michigan State University (1986–1993) and professor of education and social policy at the Harvard Graduate School of Education (1971–1986). In 1976–1977 he was a visiting professor at the Institution for Social and Policy Studies of Yale University. Cohen's current research interests include educational policy, the relation between policy and instruction, and the nature of teaching practice. His past work has included studies of the effects of schooling, various efforts to reform schools and teaching, the evaluation of educational experiments and large-scale intervention programs, and the relation between research and policy.

Kati Haycock is one of the nation's leading child advocates in the field of education. She is currently the director of the Education Trust. Established in 1992, the trust provides hands-on assistance to urban school districts and universities that want to work together to improve student achievement, kindergarten through college. Before coming to the Education Trust, Haycock was president of The Achievement Council, a statewide organization that provides assistance to teachers and principals in predominantly minority schools to improve student achievement. Haycock has also served as director of outreach and student affirmative action programs for the nine-campus University of California system.

Michael Johanek is a research associate and special advisor to the president at the College Board, and adjunct assistant professor of education at New York University, where he teaches educational history and philosophy. Prior to completing his doctorate in the Department of Philosophy and the Social Sciences at Teachers College, Columbia University, in 1995, he coordinated the College's Fellows in Teaching Program, the Urban Fellows Program, and the national Mellon Fellows Collaborative while serving as an instructor in the teacher education program. Previously, he taught high school studies for seven years in Cleveland, New York City, and in Lima, Peru. In addition to his dissertation of the history of community schooling in East Harlem, his recent publications include "Private Citizenship and School Choice," in *The Choice Controversy*, edited by Peter W. Cookson, Jr., and, with Donald Stewart, "The Evolution of College Entrance Examinations," in

The Ninety-fifth Yearbook of the National Society for the Study of Education, edited by Joan Boykoff Baron and Dennie Palmer Wolf.

Harry Judge was for fifteen years head of the Oxford University Department of Educational Studies, and remains at Oxford as a fellow of Brasenose College. Before returning to Oxford he was a high school principal for twelve years and spent part of his early career teaching in schools. He has published extensively on educational issues in Britain and the United States, and recently completed a four-year comparative study of the relationship between universities and teacher education. He is currently working on a comparative study of the impact of religious groups on educational policy.

Theodore R. Mitchell is vice chancellor of academic planning and budget for the University of California, Los Angeles. From 1992 to 1994 he was dean of the UCLA Graduate School of Education. Prior to coming to UCLA, Mitchell earned his B.A. in economics and history at Stanford University, an M.A. in history, and a Ph.D. in education, also at Stanford. He taught at Dartmouth College from 1981 to 1991, and in 1991 served as deputy to the president and provost at Stanford. Mitchell's research has focused on educational organizations from a historical perspective, with a particular interest in exploring how educational organizations in the United States have resisted or embraced change. Mitchell is active in civic organizations, serving on the executive working group of LEARN (Los Angeles Educational Alliance for Restructuring Now) and on the boards of the Los Angeles Educational Partnership, the Fund for the Community's Future, Children Now, and the UCLA Foundation.

Frank B. Murray is H. Rodney Sharp Professor in the Department of Educational Studies and the Department of Psychology at the University of Delaware, and served as dean of the College of Education between 1979 and 1995. He received his B.A. from

St. John's College in Annapolis, Maryland, and his M.A.T. and Ph.D. from Johns Hopkins University. He has worked on the editorial boards and in various other capacities for several journals in developmental and educational psychology, and is a fellow in the American Psychological Association and the American Psychological Society. Currently, he is interim president of the Holmes Partnership and former chair of its forerunner, the Holmes Group, a consortium of research universities engaged in educational reform. He was president and co-founder of the Project 30 Alliance, an organization of faculty in education and the liberal arts. Since 1994, he has been co-editor of the *Review of Educational Research* for the American Educational Research Association. In 1996 he edited *The Teacher Educator's* handbook for the American Association of Teacher Education. For his contributions to the field of child development and teacher education, he was awarded an honorary doctorate from Heriot-Watt University in Edinburgh, Scotland, in 1994.

Donald M. Stewart is president of the College Board. Prior to becoming president of the College Board, he was for ten years the sixth president of Spelman College. He came to Spelman after serving as associate dean of arts and sciences, assistant professor in the Department of City and Regional Planning, and in other posts at the University of Pennsylvania. Previously, he worked with the Ford Foundation in the Overseas Development Federation. Stewart contributes to numerous boards, including the Martin Luther King, Jr., Center for Nonviolent Social Change, Grinnell College, Teachers College at Columbia University, Committee for Economic Development, The New York Times Company, the Campbell Soup Company, the Mayo Foundation, the New York Community Trust, and others. He is also a member of the Visiting Committee to the John F. Kennedy School of Government at Harvard University. Stewart is a graduate of Grinnell College, Yale University, and Harvard's Kennedy School of Government.

Lawrence A. Torres is a Ph.D. candidate in administration at the Graduate School of Education and Information Studies, University of California, Los Angeles. He holds an M.A. and a Certificate of Advanced Study from Harvard University's Graduate School of Education. Torres graduated from Trinity College in Hartford, Connecticut, with a B.A. in history and political science. He is currently teaching in the Los Angles Unified School District's independent study school after having been both a classroom teacher and at-risk student counselor.

Higher Education and School Reform

Chapter One

Introduction: Higher Education and School Reform—A Missing Voice

P. Michael Timpane, Lori S. White

Different and distinct as they may be, schools and institutions of higher education are intimately interrelated by their missions, functions, operations, and co-dependence. They are the institutions in our society created and sustained for the primary purpose of learning, discovering, fostering, and communicating knowledge. They deal with the same population at successive stages—each level of education must respond to what the previous stage presents to it—and they deal successively with the same powerful demographic shifts in the numbers, location, and composition of the nation's students. They contend successively with changes in the kind of education for which students and society call. They strive with limited success to influence and satisfy one another by the establishment of content and performance criteria for high school graduation and college admission, as well as elaborate procedures for the transition; by the preparation in colleges and universities of almost all school teachers; and by extensive university research examining issues of young people's learning, teaching, and schooling. They share, as well, responsibilities and commitments to access and opportunity for every student. Both are powerful institutions in their community, with complex, often troubled relations with their neighbors and local clientele. How, one must ask, do they manage to have so little constructive engagement with each other?

Historically, the school-college connection has often been close, but never perfect. In the colonial and early national period, many colleges prepared their own students at grammar schools under their control or influence, sending a significant proportion of their graduates forth as preacher-teachers to carry on the traditional enterprise by founding and operating schools. In the nineteenth century, the purposes of education became gradually more secular and democratic, but the linkages remained—in Jefferson's vision of complementary missions for primary and university education in Virginia, for example, and in the early land-grant colleges' influence over the establishment of secondary schools in their states.

Such assumptions of shared purpose (under the colleges' control, of course) were shattered in the late nineteenth and early twentieth century, as Mitchell and Torres describe in Chapter Two of this volume. Colleges became universities and centers of basic and applied research; normal schools sprang up to train teachers separately; and public schools became pervasive institutions, responding to the wrenching phenomena of industrialization, immigration, and technological change. Amid such massive growth, change, and differentiation of function, schools and colleges grew apart. Developments since World War II have continued the process. The ascendancy of the research university has pulled higher education ever further away from the practical world of public schooling. The crises of the 1960s—school desegregation, integration, and the educational emphases of the War on Poverty; campus protests and violence amid swiftly expanding college enrollments—precluded any focus on issues of shared purpose between the schools and higher education. Indeed, in actions such as the uncoordinated revision downward of, first, college entrance requirements and, subsequently, high school graduation standards, the two sets of institutions sowed the seeds of the current misunderstanding and conflict over such issues as remedial courses in colleges and universities.

In the light of these historical influences on the development of schools and colleges and their educational priorities, it comes as a disappointment but hardly a surprise that for most of the past fifteen years' era of school reform, higher education has been a minor player and a missing voice, but a lurking presence nevertheless—the "dog that did not bark."

To be sure, the school reform movement has absorbed and engaged the energies of numerous commentators situated in colleges and universities. Nevertheless, it has proceeded without clear guidance or persistent intellectual or political support from the leadership of higher education at the institutional, system, or national level. There have been occasional efforts by individuals or small groups of higher education personnel—with individual college presidents providing guidance and support—but they have been minor episodes in the progress of precollegiate reform. There certainly has been nothing resembling the business community's sustained response to the problems of schools; it was notable, to say the least, that when business leaders and governors met at a "summit" on education reform in 1996, no leaders of higher education were invited to attend.

The record of the past decade suggests specific reasons why higher education has not been more widely involved in school reform:

• Higher education itself has been in a time of great crisis during the past decade. Its problems include financial stringency, increasing competition among institutions, skeptical questions from the public and politicians about the productivity and efficiency of the enterprise, and difficult adaptations to new clienteles and technologies. Add to those a growing disillusionment among students and parents springing from inexorably rising tuitions, a seemingly remote professoriate, slow progress in responding effectively to the needs of minority students or to demands for multicultural programs, and governance problems caused by restive trustees or state-system administrators.

• Health, welfare, correctional institutions, and the schools are consuming an increasingly higher percentage of state budgets through legislated or constitutionally mandated calls for resources, leaving an ever-shrinking share of state budgets for higher education, and either implicitly or explicitly pitting higher education and schools against each other in political and policy battles for state funding.

• Many of the schools' problems seem to those in higher education more societal than educational, and colleges and universities do not see themselves as being in a position to help with them. This line of thought suggests that chronic social conditions of poverty, discrimination, social instability, and just plain misery must be addressed directly before higher education—or anyone else for that matter—can realistically hope to help the schools.

• There is a great, as yet unbridged, intellectual and cultural gap between schools and higher education. The gulf can be thought of as an epistemological one between advanced academic inquiry and a practical, populist pedagogy that gives more credence to experience than it does to the findings of research. It can be seen as the distance between a predominantly upper-middle-class, historically male profession and a predominantly lower-middle-class, mostly female profession; or between high- and low-prestige occupations. However one describes this gap, the ongoing discourse across it is slight.

• There has been, until recently, little evidence that colleges and universities intended to reconsider their traditional admissions practices of emphasizing the amount of academic course taking (Carnegie Units) and standardized admissions tests. These practices contributed to rigidities in high school curricula, the development of academic tracking, a lesser concern in many schools for the education of noncollege-bound youth, and a general reluctance to modify school programs in any way that might jeopardize pupils' admission to college.

• Higher education is itself so fragmented and competitive that no across-the-board sectoral response can be generated for this or any other issue. The precollegiate system is at least equally fragmented, though along different dimensions; and the two systems have grown and are governed quite separately, even competitively.

Higher education has, in short, been preoccupied with its own problems, with little energy to spare for schools' problems. Thus beset, the typical college or university president may be, and probably is, well-meaning in his or her concern about schools but unlikely to make support for public schools a top priority. At the same time, no one among those selecting, assessing, or rewarding presidents has provided incentives or sanctions for performance in this arena.

The pity is that higher education's help has been badly needed to give clear expressions of its standards and expectations, to contribute its knowledge systematically to the development of precollegiate programs, and to provide consistent encouragement and support to the efforts of those trying to improve our schools. To be sure, colleges and universities can be erratic and condescending in their support of elementary and secondary education, but it seems unlikely that school reform efforts can be sustained without the credibility that only higher education's endorsement can provide (for example, college admission standards and university-based professional training programs for new and continuing teachers that reinforce and reflect the changes wrought by school reforms in standards, curricula, teaching, and assessment).

Moreover, higher education has a potentially great contribution to make to the advancement and improvement of precollegiate education in the form of both knowledge and political support. Higher education could greatly enhance its own standing with the public by visibly contributing its knowledge and skill to the improvement of schooling and by providing clear-cut political support for school reforms.

Growing Signs of Hope

As discouraging as prospects for a sustained and meaningful role for higher education in school reform may seem, there are growing signs of hope:

• The instances of effective collaboration are increasing, ever more rapidly, in recent years, and are becoming more ambitious and comprehensive. Academic alliances between public school teachers and higher education faculty members have grown and persisted for over a decade. On many campuses, faculties from the schools of arts and sciences and schools of education have, with encouragement from presidents and provosts, launched joint projects to encourage school improvements and policy reforms. The College Board's Equity 2000 project and the K–16 collaborations of the American Association for Higher Education have created academically focused community-based partnerships in many cities.

• Schools of education are becoming stronger and more effective, although they have a long way to go before they are as effective as they should be. In the early 1980s these schools were in a weakened state, having been through the drastic enrollment declines and staffing reductions brought about by the constriction of the teaching labor market during the 1970s. They were historically lacking in luster and prestige on their own campuses (and spending too much of their time and energy worrying about it!). Along with such other schools as nursing and social work, they had little appeal for students of the 1980s who were being lured by the siren calls of business and law. The 1990s have brought a dramatic reversal of these trends; more numerous and highly qualified applicants are seeking training for careers in education—many of them leaving other professional fields by mid-career choice or early retirement. School teaching is now seen as a worthwhile, challenging career, with modest but not disgraceful salary levels and a measure of job stability and security increasingly absent from other occupations. In this environment, schools of education have been able to raise standards and requirements, reform curricula, and enter more confidently into collaborations with their counterparts in the arts and sciences.

• The research and program design work of faculty members from schools of education have given the school-reform movement much of its knowledge base—in cognitive psychology and new knowledge-based pedagogies, in the application of organizational analysis to schools, in new assessments, and in the development of models of teaching, learning, and school performance that integrate these insights. The schools of education have also improved their own programs for the preparation of education professionals and are participating much more closely with the schools in the new forms of professional development and school restructuring that lie at the heart of contemporary hopes for school improvement. The recent report of the National Commission on Teaching and America's Future (1996), *What Matters Most: Teaching for America's Future*, further brightens prospects by placing the reform and improvement of teacher education at the heart of the nation's quest for well-qualified effective teachers in every classroom.

Overview of This Volume

Chapters Two through Four of the remaining seven chapters of this volume describe historical and contemporary contexts for the divisions between schools and higher education and some recent initiatives to bridge the historic gulf. Chapters Five through Seven search, mostly within higher education, for deep-seated reasons for frustration and hope. The final chapter is an illuminating reflection from abroad.

In Chapter Two, Theodore Mitchell and Lawrence Torres describe a historical relationship between schools and colleges that has never been one of alignment or real partnership. According to Mitchell and Torres, higher education has historically attempted to control what goes on in schools by insisting that universities hold the scientific knowledge upon which educational practice should be based. The rejection of this view by growing and newly confident teacher organizations early in this century crystallized the dramatic differences of perspective and practice that has persisted even throughout this century. Central questions raised by this history include whether higher education and schools should be thought of as part of one education system and whether it will be possible for schools and colleges to forge an equal partnership. From the perspective of systemic school reform, the fundamental question is whether and how an agenda of high standards, curricular frameworks, and institutional and professional development focused on learning outcomes might bring these institutions together in ways never previously observed, or whether the deep-seated differences between higher education and schools described by Mitchell and Torres must forever stand in the way of any hope for sustained partnerships.

In Chapter Three, Patrick Callan offers a contrasting view with his belief that higher education and schools comprise a single system. He suggests that active efforts by state governments and policymakers should span or eliminate artificial boundaries between the two. Callan sees three areas where states could and should exercise leverage to foster collaboration between higher education and schools: standards-based reform, teacher education, and assurance of access to higher education. Without state intervention, Callan believes that higher education is likely to participate only in those reforms that require minimal effort on its part. He suggests that states should use their authority not merely to prescribe a relationship between schools and higher education but to stimulate conversation and systemic thinking around issues that affect school instruction and student learning.

Kati Haycock also argues in Chapter Four that systemic reform is the appropriate way to think about the improvement of education, from the beginning of schooling through undergraduate education; in other words, K–16 systemic reform. One of her central premises is that the systemic reform movement will be derailed if colleges and universities do not participate more fully, particularly in areas such as college admissions and teacher training. Haycock reviews three waves of school–higher education partnerships—those focused on increasing minority student access to higher education, on achieving educational excellence in schools, and on preparing students for the workplace. She profiles three "systemic reform" school-college partnerships—partnerships that are more overarching than the more traditional, piecemeal partnerships involving one or two college faculty with one or two schools. She concludes with an imposing list of basic tasks that higher education must undertake to become a credible and effective force for school reform.

One of the primary educational processes linking higher education and schools is teacher training. In Chapter Five, Frank Murray proposes a restructuring of teacher education based on the efforts of the school reform movement to foster teaching for understanding (rather than solely facts and skills). Murray defines an "honest" teacher education program as one that provides mastery and understanding of the teaching field, liberal and general education, educational theory and research, modern pedagogical knowledge, and effective clinical practice. Such a program, argues Murray, cannot be delivered in one year of a graduate-level teacher education program. To develop "honest" teacher education programs, Murray calls for a reform of schools of education, including a redesign of both the undergraduate and graduate teacher education curriculum and pedagogy, new instructional settings for the delivery of teacher education, and expanded school-college partnerships. Murray also argues that an undergraduate liberal arts education is essential for imparting the knowledge, understanding, and skill that undergird all good teaching, but that it is not necessarily the milieu where prospective teachers can actually learn good teaching—a theme expanded on in Cohen's succeeding chapter. Murray's chapter raises the question, will systemic reform of teacher education as a strategy for school improvement turn out to be another case of higher education's paternalism toward schools (à la Mitchell and Torres), or will issues of teacher education be those around which schools and higher education can form mutually beneficial relationships?

In the next chapter, David Cohen provides further critical analysis of major reform proposals that seek to improve schools by changing some aspects of higher education: namely, teacher education, college admission standards, and college teaching. Cohen suggests that, of these proposals, improving college teaching is the only one that may ultimately have a significant impact on improving schools or, more specifically, improving school instruction; but he finds little reason to suppose that college teaching will improve without dramatic changes in faculty values, incentives, and experience. Thus, it is difficult to argue that higher education should be the place where better "teaching about teaching" will occur. For improvement in college teaching to be realized or valued, Cohen asserts that new research must focus on instructional quality and on teaching and learning in the disciplines throughout the university. Whereas Murray examines schools of education as higher education's vehicle for improving schools, Cohen suggests that (an unlikely) wholesale reform of higher education must occur as a precondition for higher education's being of more help to schools.

An *ecological* rather than a *systemic* framework for building higher education–school connections is proposed by Donald Stewart and Michael Johanek in Chapter Seven. Stewart and Johanek's key premise is that connections between higher education and schools should be driven by intellectual vitality—defined as the shared culture and pursuit of academic inquiry—rather than by the application of common policy concepts, like uniform standards and assessments, K–16 articulation, or other assumptions arising from systemic notions of school reform. Stewart and Johanek suggest that systemic reforms alone fail to stimulate intellectual vitality among schools, teachers, students, policymakers, and the public.

Finally, taking us beyond our examination of American higher education and schools, Harry Judge, in Chapter Eight, views the relationship of higher education and schools in the United States from an international, comparative perspective. Highlighting aspects of schools and higher education in England, France, and the United States, Judge suggests a huge irony: Only in America is there a sense that school reform can be accomplished if only the right formula (that is, systemic reform) can be found; and yet for systemic reform to be achieved in America, there must first be an educational "system." He argues that the diversity of American schools and colleges, and their governance, makes the idea of reforming an American educational system a difficult if not unreal expectation. By contrast, the very structure of schools and higher education in France and England, though different from one another, stem from a shared assumption that the central government bears the responsibility for the national educational enterprise, and thus they lend themselves more readily to education reforms that are systemic in nature. The question of defining a relationship between higher education and schools (principally secondary schools) and making a case for the involvement of higher education with schools is, according to Judge, also peculiar to the United States, stemming from the different historical development of secondary schools in Europe (where the primary influence and interest of higher education is evident) and the United States (where secondary schools are primarily within the ambit of the public schools). Judge thus suggests that American higher education's involvement in schools flows less from a fundamental interest in school reform than from higher education's fear of the loss of public support should they be perceived as ignoring the problems of schools.

Moving Forward

We are left with more questions than answers. Should higher education and schools be thought of as one system or are they fundamentally different? Should state and national governments exercise greater initiative to forge relationships between higher education and schools, and if so, how? Is systemic reform the lever needed to encourage school-college partnerships, or should these connections be driven by the pursuit of intellectual vitality? Can school reform succeed without higher education participation or reform?

While we deliberate on these important questions, we must also act. There are several steps that higher education, in particular, should take—steps that will foster education's progress without compromising any parties or prejudging the eventual answer to our quandaries:

- Raise the issue of a relationship between higher education and schools explicitly, both in the national higher education community and in the school reform arena. Reaffirmation of these connections as essential to the interests of higher education must come from college and university presidents, not directors of community affairs or deans of education. They must be long-term and accompanied by resources.

- Help schools of education to become truly professional schools akin to graduate schools of business, law, and medicine—schools that serve their professions proudly, schools that do not envy the rest of the academy or see themselves as higher education's stepchildren.

- Use schools of education, not as the exclusive instrument of higher education in the schools, but as essential elements in the success of school reform and an appropriate indication that higher education will not ignore or downplay the most central ingredient in the future of society: the basic education of the next generation of citizens.

- Strive continually to make school systems more open to, and adept and enthusiastic at, seeking appropriate assistance from their colleagues in higher education, and to help higher education to see schools as equal partners and not as children who need to be told what to do and how to do it.

- Create and strengthen nongovernmental institutions that bring the two communities together around specific collaborative agenda, ranging from community-based partnerships to academic collaborations to the development of national goals and standards.

- Extend the definition of academic scholarship to encompass the scholarships of discovery, integration, application, and

teaching and thus give greater value to collaborative work
with and for the schools (Boyer, 1994).

- Invest in improving the pedagogy of all college faculty to
  incorporate contemporary insights in the nature of adult
  learning, as well as the impact of new school performance
  standards on what college freshman should know and be able
  to do.

- Create incentives and rewards for the participation of faculty
  throughout the university in school and community partnerships. (On the challenges of succeeding in such collaborations, see Brascamp and Wergin, 1997.)

- Encourage faculty participation in the activities of professional organizations or learned societies aimed at the development of consistent, demanding curriculum content and
  standards on every level.

- Develop and expand opportunities for new substantive academic collaboration between teachers and professors—for
  example, educational quality review teams composed of
  school teachers and higher education faculty to provide informal peer review of selected aspects of both school and college
  performance; or expanded opportunities for college course-
  taking by high school students.

The path to progress will not be smooth. There is still apathy
and misunderstanding on campuses, and cynicism and anger
among school reformers and practitioners. The truth be told,
higher education has not even been asked to do much in many
communities; and perhaps for this reason, its leadership has not yet
given the issue a central place or high priority, either in rhetoric or
reality. Yet, higher education can itself be neither effective nor
equitable unless schools improve their capacity to educate all children regardless of ethnic background, socioeconomic status, or ability. We will succeed only when the members of our two estranged

communities behave, by conviction and by incentive, as though they must either hang together, or, as the saying goes, hang separately.

References

Boyer, E. *Scholarship Reconsidered*. Princeton, N.J.: Carnegie Foundation for the Advancement of Teaching, 1994.

Brascamp, L. A., and Wergin, J. F. "Forming New Social Partnerships." In W. G. Tierney (ed.), *The Responsive University: Restructuring for High Performance*. Baltimore, Md.: Johns Hopkins University Press, 1997.

National Commission on Teaching and America's Future. *What Matters Most: Teaching for America's Future*. New York: National Commission on Teaching and America's Future, 1996.

Chapter Two

"Something, But Not Very Much"

School-University Partnerships in Historical Perspective

Theodore R. Mitchell, Lawrence A. Torres

A part of the human condition is the temptation to imagine nostalgic pasts in which the vexing problems of the present were more manageable. We look to the past for historical threads we want to weave today into a full tapestry of explanation, yet the end result is often distortion and rationalization. This is particularly powerful in education, where each generation creates mythical Edens against which the present appears at best chaotic and at worst, simply wrongheaded. Thus, in thinking historically about school-university partnerships, there is a natural urge to create a past in which these relationships were natural, normal, and productive. This tendency is amplified in a policy environment that seeks precedents for making these partnerships just that: natural, normal, and mutually productive.

Indeed, looking back, one can find many incidents of mutual support, clear moments of common struggle, and significant organized efforts at connection to bolster such a view. One of the first organized efforts at partnership, the creation of the New England Association of Colleges and Preparatory Schools (now the New England Association of Schools and Colleges), began in 1884 and brought together college faculty with counterparts in the academies and high schools. The aims of the Association reflect many of the goals educators hope to achieve through contemporary partnerships:

the professionalization of teaching, higher standards for student achievement, and reciprocal exchanges of expertise. On the surface, these and other efforts lend credence to the existence of a neglected tradition of joint action between the two "sectors" of the educational economy. Yet, however tempting, creating a past that emphasizes a lost tradition of collaboration would be dangerously sanguine, for such a history would both miss the underlying structural issues and, in the present context, minimize the nature and extent of the changes necessary in both sectors to make partnerships truly come alive.

From their beginnings, relationships between higher education and the schools have been typified by indifference punctuated by mistrust, marred by antagonism if not outright conflict. Speaking at the conclusion of the twentieth annual meeting of the New England Association in 1904, one of the organization's founders, William C. Collar, rose to address the membership. "I am sorry to say it," lamented Collar, "but my conviction is today that the chasm that separates the schools and the colleges is as wide and deep as it ever was." The issues were fundamental. Though always polite, the college men who participated in the meetings seemed, to Collar, to listen with "benignant condescension," and "partial amusement." Their aim, throughout, he felt, was "to grant, if they could, something, but not very much" (quoted in Krug, 1964, p. 126).

Today, a century and a decade after the founding of the nation's first school/college association, there are many, mostly school people, who would echo Collar's assessments. Indeed, it was during the period of Collar's work with the Association, roughly the 1880s until shortly before the First World War, that the fundamental structure of the relationship between schools and universities emerged, one that amplified distinctions between the two sectors of the educational economy and that continues to shackle efforts at partnership today.

Only by understanding the origins of the structures of thought, action, and organization that prevent closer and more authentic collaboration can we begin to alter present relationships, and thus create the kinds of mutually supporting partnerships that are crucial to the improvement, indeed survival, of both schools and higher education. Without such an understanding we are likely to create prescriptions that address symptoms, not causes, and continue the merry-go-round ride that pits schools and universities against each other.

Schools and Colleges in a State of Becoming

Fundamental to the historical distance between schools and colleges are the decidedly different origins of the two major sectors of the education industry, beginnings that seem to belie our present belief (and rhetoric) that schools and colleges make up a single industry or share a common identity. This later notion would have been strange, certainly, to the leaders of the colonial colleges and to the grammar school teachers of the early republic.

Jefferson, the "father of the free schooling movement," saw education as the single way to continue the democratic revolution. Though the former president never outlined a comprehensive theory of education, he saw that a republic must have a citizenry prepared to make intelligent decisions regarding their governmental systems. An educated populous would enable the common people to select qualified leaders, effectively interact with their government, and pursue their expected destiny (Heslop, 1969, p. 88).

Interestingly, Jefferson, contrary to his attested democratic ideals, was worried about the day-to-day operations of the school falling into the hands of the local officials or the masses. He envisioned a "middleman," some agent appointed by an enlightened politician, actually to control the curriculum and daily operations of the school.

Attempting to create a system of enlightened paternalism, Jefferson saw this new schooling adventure, one primarily consisting of six elementary grades followed by college entrance, to be used by those of wealth and prestige, those who would naturally be the next generation's leaders. "The only people capable of . . . leading are those who are natural aristocrats—those who possess extraordinarily strong powers of reason, morals, and taste" (Heslop, 1969, pp. 88–89). He did believe, however, that once in a very great while, the sons of working-class people could show such promise that they, too, should be allowed to enter the great university at public expense. In his 1779 bill to the Virginia Legislature, he said: "At the end of six years' instruction, one half are to be discontinued and the other half, who shall be chosen for the superiority of their parts and disposition, are to be sent and continued three years in the study of such sciences as they shall choose, at William and Mary College" (Conant, 1962, p. 4).

Perhaps Jefferson's elitist stand was a way to appease a public not yet ready for mass public schooling, the public, incidentally, choosing to identify itself as the wealthy who would be forced to pay for this large entitlement program. The measure was handily defeated in the Virginia Legislature. Jefferson tried again, this time asking for a three-year public schooling act. The wealthy, knowing their sons were already safely educated by tutors and private academies, rejected this bill as well.

Aside from Jefferson's ideal construction, and the odd Boston Latin School, the 'system' of educational institutions in the colonies and the early republic was discontinuous and chaotic. Enrollment in grammar schools was episodic and attendance more so (see Kaestle and Vinovskis, 1980, p. 46, and Cremin, 1961, ch. 4). Individuals moved into higher education from a wide range of preceding experiences, sometimes including time at a local grammar school, sometimes not. Greek and Latin were the limiting prerequisites for entry into the colonial colleges well into the nineteenth century. For most interested applicants, this meant time with a tutor or time spent in a private academy (Krug, 1964, pp. 1–7). That and a well-placed reference letter from an influential 'friend' allowed easy entrance into most universities.

Close relationships developed between these colleges and many of the academies, as "feeder" relationships developed and deepened. Academies provided training that prepared students for the entrance examinations to their patron college. In return, the college often provided the academies with a stream of young teachers on their way to the law, the ministry, or simply between terms (Hawkins, 1972, pp. 224–225).

These feeder relationships were mutually beneficial. The academies recruited students with some assurance that they would be prepared at the end of their course for entrance into college and enjoyed a steady supply of instructors. For their part, the colleges had stabilized the quality of their applicants and were able to maintain enrollments and the perception of admission standards. Of course, enrollment for both never reached even the numbers of most small private colleges in existence today. Presaging the future, these feeder relationships depended upon the academies' willingness to organize instruction around the entrance requirements of colleges. In these early years, this meant elementary training in the classical languages. In later years, this issue was to become more complicated and more confounding for colleges and schools alike.

More chaotic was the proliferation of "colleges" throughout the land with widely divergent curricula, requirements, and aspirations. Some were little more than grammar schools, others rivaled the colonial colleges. It was among these institutions that the line of demarcation between higher education and grammar school was blurred. Normal schools, begun in the early nineteenth century, contributed to these blurred boundaries.

There also was a problem of the purpose of colleges. Often they were very closed societies, admitting students for very specific purposes. Colleges were often based around frameworks such as religion, military, or teacher training. Yet one could easily become a preacher, soldier, or teacher by simply apprenticing oneself to the desired occupation.

Altenbaugh and Underwood (1990, p. 136) have described teacher training in the nineteenth century as "historically diffuse." Indeed, during the first two-thirds of the nineteenth century, preparation for teaching, like preparation for higher education, was unregulated, chaotic, and locally determined. Enrollment growth during the middle decades of the 1800s demanded an increasing supply of trained teachers, a demand that could not be met by these informal, haphazard means. To address the need, local and state superintendents, as well as ministers and religious societies, created teachers' institutes, demonstration and training schools, and, finally, normal schools. Normal schools, much like the academies that prepared students for the colonial colleges, provided a modicum of appropriate training to women desiring a career in elementary school teaching. Early proponents, including New England reformer Calvin Stowe, believed, as Jurgen Herbst puts it, that "normal schools and their students belonged to the world of the common school, not to the sphere of secondary or collegiate education" (Herbst, 1980, p. 224). In keeping with this understanding, early normal departments were connected with the common school, established either privately or in connection with a city school system. In every instance, public normal schools were operated under the auspices of the state school superintendent, not by universities or colleges. Yet even these distinctions were soon blurred.

The first public normal school, begun by Horace Mann and led by Cyrus Pierce, opened in Lexington, Massachusetts in 1839. Almost immediately, Pierce found, to his chagrin, that more than a few of his charges had no intention of becoming teachers. Instead, for them the opportunity that normal school training provided was that of higher education. Across the country, as Altenbaugh and Underwood note, normal schools became a primary avenue for higher education for young women, despite the stated intentions of the institutions (Altenbaugh and Underwood, 1990, pp. 138–142). Simply because of the lack of alternate, authentic higher education opportunities, normal schools began to be regarded as higher education. Unintentionally, at least in the eye of the educational establishment, normal schools had become both fish and fowl.

The development and rapid expansion of the high school further confounded efforts to draw lines between different forms of institutionalized education and precipitated change in the relationships among academies, colleges, universities, and normal schools. From the beginning, high schools, like normal schools, took on a multitude of contradictory tasks. They provided additional work in literature, mathematics, and science to grammarians on their way into commerce; some provided classical training for young men on their way to college; and some provided a normal course for young women headed back into elementary school classrooms. To some, high schools were to become "the people's college," and for a select few they were to become the people's way to college. Over time, resolution of that contradiction would define in large measure an array of relationships between schools and higher education. More immediately, though, high schools overlapped with the academies and the normal schools in significant ways. In the East, with its well-established academies and normal schools, this overlap was pronounced and uncomfortable.

Among those who were irritated by the "high school question" was Charles Eliot, president of Harvard College and widely considered a leader of reform in the arena of higher education. Eliot first entered the debate over the high school in 1873 in a speech to the Department of Superintendence of the National Education Association (NEA). For the next thirty years, Eliot's arguments changed, and as they did, Eliot both shaped and reflected the debate over the relationship between schools and colleges. Perhaps no individual was as important in shaping the ultimate structure of the relationships between schools and universities than was Eliot. As the historian of the high school, Edward Krug, put it: "For at least a quarter of a century . . . discussion of public schooling, and of high schools in particular, was to involve being for or against something Eliot had said" (Krug, 1964, p. 18).

In 1873 what Eliot said was that public high schools should not aspire to preparatory training: "The first work of public schools is not now to fit for college." Instead, "their work is to train their pupils in English, in mathematics, and in classics, a little, up to their seventeenth year" (quoted in Hawkins, 1972, p. 225). For

Eliot and his supporters, the academies suited well for preparatory training.

Eliot's was not the only voice, however. President James McCosh of Princeton rose to rebut Eliot and sounded the argument that was to prevail, and prevail in the end with Eliot's leadership: "We want schools such that there shall be no poor boy in the country who shall not have within a few miles of him such a school as will enable him to go on to the highest place" (quoted in Hawkins, 1972, p. 226). In the West, the view expressed by McCosh had dominated debates over the high school from the beginning and had shaped the development of relationships between the public schools and the public universities established under the Morrill Act. There, with fewer traditional patterns in place, educators and the public created a system of institutional relationships that, on paper at least, brought Jefferson's vision of a system of schooling, well articulated from the early years through the university, into focus. But here, too, development of the high school created confusion, in this case with the normal schools of the region, and set into motion changes with long-lasting consequences for the relationships between schools and colleges.

In the Midwest and West, high schools and normal schools developed simultaneously and sometimes in competition. As they matured, high schools incorporated elementary school teacher training into the curriculum and competed directly with the emerging normal schools. At times, the process worked in reverse.

In 1858, the Wisconsin legislature opened a normal school in Platteville, attempting both to increase the number of teachers for the elementary schools of the region and to meet the residents' long expressed desire for a public high school. According to Jeff Wasserman, "That citizens regarded an academy or high school as more important than a professional school for training teachers was apparent from the start." Many students, male as well as female, enrolled in order to gain a secondary education. That the course of study was organized around teacher training seems to have been irrelevant (quoted in Altenbaugh and Underwood, 1990, p. 142).

The response of the normal school at Platteville, though, was not irrelevant, nor was it atypical for the region. Faculty at Platteville expanded the curriculum to include traditional high school subjects. Soon, teacher training had become marginalized. It was a trend that was to be repeated on a larger scale during the first decades of the twentieth century.

By the beginning of the 1880s, the informal dynamics that ruled interaction between institutions and between institutions and individuals had become, in the space between elementary school and college, a cacophony of competing organizational forms. The roles of academies and high schools became less and less clear as high schools offered multiple courses of study, including a college preparatory course. The debate centered on an education based upon "local" needs versus the Jeffersonian enlightened citizen ideal. The roles of normal schools and high schools became similarly confused. Apart and above, colleges and universities were undergoing their own transformation, which included the rejection of the traditional classical course of undergraduate study for a more diverse combination of electives and requirements. More significantly, at least for the future of relations with schools, was the welcome acceptance of the university ideal of professional as well as liberal education. (This included both the private institutions, like Cornell, Harvard, and Johns Hopkins, and the land grant institutions. See Veysey, 1965, ch. 8.) Added to this mix were the changes in society that put pressure on all American social institutions, including schools, colleges, and universities.

Increasing levels of immigration, the rapid concentration of population, centralization of wealth, and seemingly unending acceleration of industrialization threatened the traditional distribution of power and authority. These changes, felt most keenly in America's urban centers, threatened a powerful coalition of interests, including displaced elites, industrialists, and political professionals, who sought ways to reassert the kind of order and stability they believed necessary for the functioning of society and through which their interests would be protected and preserved. The progressive movement was an effort by these groups to create a counterbalance to the entropy forces of the age. In what Robert Wiebe called the "search for order," schools and universities were both tools and targets of progressive reform (see Wiebe, 1967; Cremin, 1961; Tyack, 1974).

The progressive era has been regarded rightly as a watershed in the history of education. New approaches to teaching and the curriculum, based on the emerging psychology and philosophy of John Dewey and Edward Thorndike, reflected a newly self-conscious effort to make education work to develop mental capacity as well as to inculcate behavioral norms. A new consensus about administrative efficiency and professional control claimed to place educational decisions in the hands of experts rather than local politicians. What united the educational progressives and the administrative progressives was their faith in expertise and science in shaping education (though Dewey would later protest against this very same scientific movement). In this way, as in many others, the university became more central to schooling than it had ever been. In the development of this new role, the basic patterns of the relationship between schools and colleges that persist today—patterns reflective of Collar's "something, but not very much"—emerged and were embedded in practice.

Progressivism and the Structuring of School-University Relations

As early as 1881, in his annual report, President Barnard of Columbia College was able to articulate this new role for colleges and universities: "Education is nowhere [in America] treated as a science, and nowhere is an attempt made to expound its true philosophy." Barnard set a clear path for Columbia. By creating a "department embracing the history, theory, and practice of education, Columbia College may very properly make an attempt to supply the serious defect in the educational system of our country."

The aim of such a department would be to "reach the teachers of the public schools of the city of New York and its vicinity . . . for at present they have, as a rule, no more adequate knowledge of their task, and certainly have no preparation for it. We may except a few, who have had the training of the normal schools, but even for such it is doubtful how far that is sufficient" (Barnard, *Report 1881–1882*, quoted in Whittemore, 1970, pp. 30–31). Barnard's patronizing desire to create at Columbia a department in which the science of education could be systematically discovered and transmitted to those who would work in schools typified the impulse of institutions of higher education for direct contact with secondary and elementary schools.

In Chicago, this impulse led several years later to the creation of a school of education and a laboratory school whose purpose was "to train competent specialists for the broad and scientific treatment of educational problems." John Dewey, writing about the development of his own department at Chicago, echoed Barnard's assumptions, asserting, "It is obvious, without argument, that this higher type of training must be undertaken for the most part, if it is to be done in America at all, by universities" (quoted in Storr, 1966, p. 296). This notion, that colleges were the seat of knowing, expanded during the progressive era as the importance of science as a way of understanding righting the world expanded beyond the laboratory and factory as universities claimed themselves to be the place where science was best served.

Ironically, the early 1880s marked the time when school leaders began to seek actively interaction with universities and colleges. At the 1883 meeting of the Massachusetts Classical and High School Teachers, their seventeenth such gathering, the membership passed two resolutions. The first stated that "in the opinion of this Association the want of understanding and effective cooperation between the teachers of the preparatory and high schools and the faculties of the colleges is a serious evil." The second suggested that "a meeting of delegates of this Association with representatives of New England Colleges would be productive of good" (quoted in Krug, 1964, p. 1). The outgrowth of these resolutions would be the creation of the New England Association of Colleges and Preparatory Schools in 1884. Over the next ten years, school/college associations emerged in the middle states and Maryland and in the north central states. Although all of these did bring together school people and faculty from colleges and universities, as Collar concluded, the results were mixed, indeed (Krug, 1964, p. 127).

These mixed results owed to the rapidly solidifying consensus among university and college leaders regarding their relations with schools. If university people listened to school people with "partial amusement," as Collar suggests, it was because university faculty readily subscribed to Barnard's notion that they should be the experts and that universities should do the "science" upon which educational practice would be based. In this context, what is remarkable is that Collar found university faculty who were willing to listen to school people at all!

Essential to understanding the dynamic that shaped this expert-based paternalism is the ubiquitous role into which university leaders asserted their faculties. The emerging role of scientific expert went hand in hand with the professionalization of university faculty. Speaking to the "newness" of academic expertise, historian Steven Diner argues that "the first generation of academic professionals lived in a world that did not depend upon their expertise" (Diner, 1980, p. 8). Before they could play a full role in progressive America, faculty and their presidents had to create markets for academic products: training and research.

At the same time that they were arguing for the importance of their institutions in the area of education, university presidents were making the same arguments in virtually every other professional domain—from law to medicine, business, engineering, and social work (Murphy, 1990, p. 35; see also Noble, 1979). The era saw the proliferation of professional schools and the rise of the university form in the United States. Land-grant institutions that had limped through the 1870s found voice and legitimacy in the 1880s and 1890s as the elite and relatively ancient institutions of the northeast added schools of business, medicine, agriculture, mining, and education. The founding at the end of the century first of Cornell and then of Stanford as universities dedicated to liberal arts in service of practical knowledge, epitomized the change internal to higher education during the progressive period. Like their German counterparts, the American university was to be an engine for the creation of useful knowledge disseminated by a faculty of experts to a grateful society.

Sometimes, however, the society was not immediately grateful, nor responsive. In 1885, Nicholas Murray Butler, soon to become a major force in solidifying the dynamic of school-college relations, complained with a certain innocent wonder that although "our college presidents recognize our need (for university-trained teachers) governing boards do not seem to carry out their recommendations" (Butler, 1885, pp. 529–530). Diner's point seems to hold. Universities in the 1880s and 1890s needed first and foremost to make a market for the expertise they offered for sale. In education, many did this in the most direct way possible: by taking control of the schools themselves. The idea was not to dirty their hands on the mundane day-to-day workings of any single classroom or institution, but rather to command the political structure from which school power emanated.

In 1887, Nicholas Murray Butler was appointed to the board of education for the state of New Jersey. In his position, Butler relentlessly called for university training for teachers, centralization of control over schools in the hands of professionally trained superintendents, and control of corrupt practices. His position as a member of the board was not unique. Many college faculty took positions along with others of the progressive elite on boards of education, as they did on the boards of hospitals and businesses, in order to be a conduit for university expertise (Diner, 1980, pp. 86, 99). Charles Eliot served on the Boston School Committee; Daniel Gilman and his two successors, Ira Remsen and Frank Goodnow, served on the Baltimore Board. Even the taciturn and distant Abbott Lawrence Lowell, who succeeded Eliot as president of Harvard, served a term on the Boston School Committee. This was market-making at its best. When problems arose, as they often did during the era, university presidents were at hand to suggest which of their stable of experts might be able to lend a hand.

Ironically, the boards of trustees were most wary of their presidents taking on work with schools. When William Rainey Harper wrote to a board member asking whether he should stand for reappointment to the Chicago Board of Education, the board member replied with forthrightness, "While you might be able after two or three years of distasteful work, to succeed in carrying out your wishes as to a closer contact between the University and the public schools, yet it seems the game would not be worth the powder . . . you cannot handle dirt without soiling your clothes" (quoted in Diner, 1980, p. 82). Yet whatever the risks, real or imagined, university presidents of the 1880s and 1890s served with great energy on school boards throughout the land. Others, like Andrew Draper, E. Benjamin Andrews, and Ernest Caroll Moore, moved between college leadership and the leadership of school systems. Some, overlapping both previous groups, took up leadership positions within the National Education Association, and in that group's formative years, shaped its policies and practices (see Whittemore, 1970, ch. 6; Tyack, 1974, pp. 100–140; Hawkins, 1972, ch. 8; Diner, 1980, ch. 4; Murphy, 1990, p. 50). At the end of the period, James Russell was moved to compare these leaders, Eliot, Lowell, Butler, and Barnard, with the captains of industry: "They were the Rockefellers, the Carnegies, the Morgans of our profession, when giants towered over the common herd . . . they were the feudal barons of the pedagogical realm, the educational elite of the golden age of rugged individualism" (quoted in Tyack, 1974, p. 137). In some senses they deserved Russell's description. In particular, they deserved comparison with men who were as effective as they, not only at building markets, but at gaining control of them.

This control developed as institutions as well as individuals responded to the new "scientification" of education. Universities emerged during the progressive era as the dominant player in education partly because of a social epistemology, which they did much to build, that put scientific expertise in their hands, to be spread among the professionally illiterate in medicine, law, business, and engineering. They also came to dominate because of the energy of their leaders in creating bases of power within the big-city school boards. In parallel with shaping this demand, universities built capacity to meet it, and build they did, creating professional schools in a wide range of disciplines. In education, the final form of these sub-units, departments, colleges, and schools of education reified the structure of relationships between higher and elementary secondary education.

At Columbia, the idea of a course of study for teachers became a recurring theme in Barnard's speeches and reports in the early 1880s. Taking up the challenge at Barnard's urging, Nicholas Murray Butler made the establishment of a professional school of education, in which the science of education could be discovered and taught, a crusade. In writings that flooded the pages of the popular press and dominated the *Educational Review,* Butler pressed his cause. More locally, he worked from his platform as a member of the philosophy department at Columbia to convince colleagues of the importance of a scientific approach to education.

Butler's break came when he was named to head the Industrial Education Association. With Barnard's support, he quickly moved to transform the IEA's professional training arm into the New York College for the Training of Teachers. Butler was clear to contrast this effort from others with which it might be confused. "Normal schools," he wrote with insufficiently disguised disdain, "are academies or high schools with a slight infusion of pedagogic instruction." In contrast, the New York College developed a full course of inquiry into the history, philosophy, and methods of education. Only this latter, scientific approach to training, Butler believed, could provide the schools with the personnel they needed (Butler, 1888, pp. 11–12).

Butler and Barnard, along with Barnard's successor Seth Low, worked during the early 1890s to amalgamate the New York College for the Training of Teachers with Columbia College. The trustees were reluctant. Their fear, and a telling one, was that the inclusion of a teachers' college, enrolling primarily female students, in a university confederation would make it far too likely that women would soon be demanding attendance in the College itself. This gender overlay, in which the communities of liberal learning, the colleges at least, were still largely male enclaves, did much to maintain the separation of schools from higher education. More-over, the bias in many of the established colleges against women caused the development of professional schools of education to lag behind those of other professions into which the new universities inserted themselves. (See Whittemore, 1970, ch. 2, 3. This is not to deny the importance of women's higher education during the period or the experience of institutions, especially the land grant universities that were coeducational from the beginning.)

Despite these and other reservations, the New York College for the Training of Teachers became Teachers College, Columbia, in November 1894. There to officiate were several "feudal barons" of the educational empire. Eliot, now a national figure in school reform thanks to his leadership of the NEA's Committee of Ten, gave an enthusiastic endorsement to Butler's ideal of scientific training. Daniel Coit Gilman of Johns Hopkins spoke of the mission of the new universities in America to bring science to bear on a whole host of social problems, including but not limited to education (Murphy, 1990, p. 28; Whittemore, 1970, ch. 3).

In Chicago, a similar movement was under way at the new University of Chicago. Chicago's founding president, William Rainey Harper, was convinced that the university needed a professional division of education, and he recruited John Dewey and later Francis Parker to realize that goal. Harper's successor, Henry Pratt Judson, was clear about the goal of such professional endeavors across the intellectual spectrum: "In a great city with its crowded population, the limits of a university's duties are to be conceived as coterminous with the limits of the city itself. In other words, the university should not be content with the discovery of scientific truth, which may have direct bearing upon the city life, but should be especially industrious in the investigation and dissemination of such forms of truth as are directly related to the city" (quoted in Diner, 1980, p. 19).

In New York and in Chicago, Presidents Butler and Harper, aided by their faculties, lost no time in disseminating their "forms of truth" to the agencies in charge of directing public schooling. In so doing they set a tone for future relationships between universities and the public schools, relationships in which universities spoke and schools listened.

Harper introduced proposals to his colleagues on the board of education that would require teachers to receive some college training in order to obtain or renew their teaching certificates. Certainly self-interested, but also clearly focused on the need to bestow scientific findings on the Windy City's teaching force, Harper was successful in his effort. Teachers, though, thwarted Harper by enrolling in courses at the Art Institute. One teacher responded dismissively to the whole idea of college training, arguing to the board that "learning how to teach from a college education is like learning how to cook from a cookbook" (Murphy, 1990, p. 30).

In New York, a Columbia-led group fought for over a decade to centralize control over New York's elementary and high schools, normal schools, and universities under a single state commissioner appointed by a small and carefully chosen board of regents. Butler, the bill's primary author, worked tirelessly on its behalf. Opponents called Butler and the Columbia interests "high-toned namby-pambys" and kept the bill from passage until 1904. After one such defeat in the state senate in 1895, the *New York Times* editorialized, "The fear of antagonizing the school teachers, whose opposition was purely of a selfish character, forced the Senate Cities Commerce Committee to report the measure unfavorably" (April 25, 1895). In 1904 the unification bill passed, and shortly thereafter, Butler's longtime friend Andrew Draper became the first commissioner of education in New York.

Important in both Chicago and New York was the emergence of a structure of intellectual colonialism of elementary and secondary education by higher education. (This construction has influenced the way we talk about the relationship between higher education and elementary/secondary education. Steven Diner, historian of Butler's Columbia, even titled his chapter on schools, "Control of the Public Schools." See Diner, 1980, p. 76.) This, in turn, created a pattern of opposition between the university reformers and the teachers. However well intended, the university's attempt to force their expertise upon teachers naturally resulted in resentment and mistrust. Although universities had done a fine job of building a market for their new "science" among political elites and policymakers, they failed to convince teachers. The hope with which Massachusetts secondary school teachers had looked upon association with higher education faculty waned by the end of the century, to be replaced by a kind of mutual enmity.

More and more meetings between teachers and professors ended in strife and deep intellectual conflict. One, held in 1896, ended abruptly after a representative from Boys High School in Brooklyn declared: "During the last two hours . . . each of the speakers have taken the trouble to state that they know little or nothing about secondary schools. This is a point upon which I am sure we can all agree . . . they [college faculty] state that they know but little of secondary school work. That saves me the trouble of proving it" (quoted in Krug, 1964, p. 125).

The comment reflects more than wounded egos or battles over turf. What it epitomized was a full-scale conflict over the source of legitimate knowledge about education. Forced to confront an expansionist university faculty, secondary and elementary school faculty for the first time began to define themselves as a profession, ironically in opposition to those who sought to "professionalize" the field through the application of scientific knowledge. In contrast, teachers began, in meetings such as these and in the sessions of the NEA, to assert the primacy of craft knowledge and of the importance of distancing themselves from the encroaching universities. As the power of the universities grew, this became less and less possible. Two moments, in particular, define the rise of intellectual colonialism during the progressive era.

The first, Charles Eliot's leadership of the NEA Committee of Ten on Secondary School Studies, asserted the dominance of colleges and universities upon the curriculum of the high school. Eliot's early position, that academies were the rightful place for preparatory studies and high schools the "peoples' colleges," changed during the decade of the 1880s. In an address to the NEA annual convention in 1890 entitled "The Gap Between Schools and Colleges," he argued that high schools should increase their ability to prepare students for college and that colleges should drive high school curriculum through their admissions requirements (Hawkins, 1972, p. 231). The speech was anathema to school people but resonant with the views of Butler and others of the progressive elite.

By 1892 the pressure to do something about the high school question had become unbearable. The National Council of the NEA, dominated by university presidents, university faculty, and big-city superintendents, decided to appoint a policy committee to study the issue and make recommendations. Butler, working openly, secured Eliot's appointment as the head of the Committee of Ten. He and Eliot, in turn, selected the other members and the members of task forces to study the major curricular areas. Of the one hundred individuals involved in the project, seventy-three were either university men, headmasters of prestigious private schools, or superintendents of major cities (see Wesley, 1957, ch. 6; Hawkins, 1972, ch. 8; Krug, 1964, ch. 3).

Not surprisingly, the recommendations of the Committee were focused on making high schools more immediately relevant to the needs of colleges and universities. Recommendations regarding structure as well as pedagogy sought to make secondary education more like that found in the nation's leading colleges and universities. High schools should offer an undifferentiated curriculum, but one based on work appropriate for the college bound. Like other Eliot products, this one was greeted with heated debate, a "deluge of discussion," Andrew White of Princeton called it (quoted in Krug, 1964, p. 67).

Augustus Nightingale, Assistant Superintendent in Chicago, led the charge of the school people, raising again the issue of legitimate knowledge. "One of the wonders of the age," he began, "is that this committee was so unanimous upon every subject and every phase of every subject, upon every grade of work except that in which the majority of the committee had had any experience" (quoted in Krug, 1964, p. 67). Even within higher education, the response was mixed. G. Stanley Hall opposed the Committee's recommendations as securing college domination over the high schools (Krug, 1964, p. 84).

In the end, the Report of the Committee of Ten did two things. First, it did lead to implementation of a more broadly discipline-based mode of study in high schools. In this it achieved Eliot's goal of making high schools more relevant to and better preparation for college. It also brought secondary schools in line with higher education and curtailed alternative possibilities for an institution that, as we have seen, had unclear and overlapping goals as late as the 1870s. Edgar Wesley, historian of the NEA, argues that the effect of the Report was to "halt the experimentation in the high school and stop all attempts to create a new institution" (Wesley, 1957, pp. 73–78; also Whittemore, 1970, p. 96). These attempts would continue, of course, in the many university laboratory schools, institutionalized representations of the role of universities as the source of scientific knowledge about teaching and learning.

This conflict over the soul of the high school was played out in the second defining moment of the era, the creation of the College Entrance Examination Board. Long a hobbyhorse of Eliot's, Butler made the standardization of college admissions requirements a crusade. He began by urging his own faculty at Columbia to establish a board in 1893, but they refused. In speech after speech to audience after audience, Butler raised the issue. Finally, in a speech before the Middle States Association of Colleges and Schools in 1899, with Eliot and other sympathetic university presidents in attendance, Butler secured a hearing.

The pivotal moment in the debate came when the president of Lafayette College rose to explain his discomfort at being forced to accept someone else's standard for student admission. Eliot chose to respond, and in an oft-quoted phrase, assured his colleague that Lafayette College "may, if it so chooses . . . admit only such students as cannot pass the examination. No one proposes," he concluded, "to deprive Lafayette College of that privilege" (quoted in Krug, 1964, pp. 148–149). Laughter, and affirmative votes, carried the day and the College Entrance Examination Board was established.

The Board, although not prescribing curriculum, quickly became the template by which high school curricula were shaped and against which school, as well as individual, success was measured. As it spread from the middle states to the Northeast and the West, the CEEB further served to bring secondary education into line with higher education and to reinforce the pattern of colonialism that typified progressive era relationships between schools and universities.

Reaction and Aftermath

The ascendancy of "scientific education" and the intellectual colonialism of the universities was not without its opponents, or without their effect. As secondary schools and universities came closer together, the friction between them increased, intellectually and politically. In 1898, Chicago's mayor refused to reappoint William Rainey Harper to the board of education, citing the view of teachers and some members of the public that Harper was trying to make the high schools into "feeders of the Chicago University" (Diner, 1980, p. 85). In a measure seeking to isolate universities from the training of teachers, Chicago teachers in 1903 nearly won a monopoly for Cook County Normal School in granting teaching certificates in the city of Chicago. Only massive lobbying by Harper and his friends defeated the measure at the board (Diner, 1980, p. 80).

But the most telling opposition occurred within the NEA. Begun in 1857, the NEA might have been a place where university leaders and school people could work together. Indeed, the membership was quite mixed. However, early in its history, the academic elite, Eliot, Butler, and their colleagues had gained control of the organization and used the NEA as a vehicle for asserting the importance of higher education in debates over elementary and secondary schools. Beginning at the turn of the century, teachers waged a struggle to wrest control of the organization away from the leaders of higher education.

Matters came to a head in 1910, when teacher leaders nominated Ella Flagg Young to succeed James Y. Joyner, president of the University of Georgia, as president of the NEA. (For more on Young, see Tyack, 1974, part V, ch. 5). Katherine Blake, a teacher from New York, gave one of the nominating speeches on Young's behalf. In her speech, she raised again the issue of gender, ever important in the structuring of school-university relationships: "You men have been working for years in this organization while we have been taking meekly and quietly the seat in the back of the room. We have come here year after year, many of us, paid our money, and listened, and it may seem to you surprising, but now we ask to be heard" (quoted in Whittemore, 1970, p. 104). And heard they were. After the parliamentary maneuvering and rules tests, Ella Flagg Young was elected president of the NEA.

The result was dramatic. Butler railed against the election in the pages of the *Educational Review,* allowing himself to be "shocked by the exhibitions of office-seeking, wire-pulling, and petty politics" (quoted in Whittemore, 1970, p. 105). In the end, however, the university men withdrew from the NEA, leaving the organization to the teachers who had done so much and been recognized with so little.

Over the course of the decade, the distance between universities and the schools grew ever greater, driven in part by a range of innovations crafted by university psychologists and administrative specialists. These innovations were bellwethers of the broader scientification of education that grew from the interest of some educational progressives to rationalize and make the operation of schools more efficient by tailoring courses of study to meet the imputed needs of broad categories of students. The Vocational Education Act of 1917 sought to focus high schools on the preparation of a nearly fully industrialized economy and to create differentiated programs within and across schools. The NEA's Committee on the Reorganization of Secondary Education reified the differentiation movement in its *Cardinal Principles* issued in 1918. In the *Principles*, a focus on the primary objectives of health, fundamental intellectual processes, worthy home membership, citizenship, ethical character, the development of vocational skills, and the worthy use of leisure time left little room for the kind of universal academic preparation advocated by Eliot and the Committee of Ten. Even this growing distance between schools and universities bore the familiar pattern of school-university relations, with university faculty taking the lead in developing the rationale and the instruments for the tracking of students and for the creation of differentiated schools and programs.

In many ways, the teacher takeover of the NEA, followed by the development of more precise and distinct roles for the American high school crystallized in the *Cardinal Principles*, represented the end of the progressive era struggle over the definition of school-university relations. After a period of engagement, typified by the colonialism of the universities, schools and universities retreated back into their separate camps. Yet despite the retreat, interactions, when they occurred, or when we initiate them today, are structured by the fundamental logic of the progressive era, a logic that juxtaposes the power of science held by universities against the oppositional legitimacy within schools of the craft knowledge developed through experience.

From the universities' point of reference, it is not their engagement in education, but their engagement in scientific inquiry that made faculty essential to the improvement of educational practice. This different skill, not any similar functions that might be observed, remains the defining characteristic of school-college relations as they were forged during the progressive era.

From the schools' point of reference, it is not their engagement with disciplines, but their engagement with children that both defines and legitimates their craft. This skill, honed through practice inaccessible to university faculty, remains the defining oppositional logic in relations with universities.

It is perhaps fitting to end with Eliot, who in 1920, in the waning days of the progressive era, attempted to summarize his accomplishments at a dinner given in honor of the twentieth anniversary of the Graduate School of Education at Harvard: "We have successfully demonstrated in the course of the last fifty years that improvements in education come from the top" (Powell, 1980, p. 20).

It is no wonder, then, that efforts to talk about interrelationships, shared students, and curricular cohesion have failed to persuade. Nothing will succeed in bringing schools and colleges closer together, in breaking the inbred paternalism of university faculty and the similarly inbred skepticism of school people, until we thoroughly alter our notions of expertise and scientific truth.

References

Altenbaugh, R. J., and Underwood, K. "The Evolution of Normal Schools." In J. I. Goodlad, R. Soder, and K. A. Sirotnik (eds.), *Places Where Teachers Are Taught*. San Francisco: Jossey-Bass, 1990.

Conant, J. B. *Thomas Jefferson and the Development of American Public Education*. Berkeley: University of California Press, 1962.

Cremin, L. *The Transformation of the Schools: Progressivism in American Education*. New York: Knopf, 1961.

Diner, S. J. *A City and Its Universities: Public Policy in Chicago, 1892–1919*. Chapel Hill: University of North Carolina Press, 1980.

Hawkins, H. *Between Harvard and America: The Educational Leadership of Charles W. Eliot*. New York: Oxford University Press, 1972.

Herbst, J. "Nineteenth Century Normal Schools in the United States: A Fresh Look." *History of Education*, 1980, 9, 219–227.

Heslop, R. D. *Thomas Jefferson and Education*. New York: Random House, 1969.

Kaestle, C., and Vinovskis, M. *Education and Social Change in Nineteenth Century Massachusetts*. Cambridge, England: Cambridge University Press, 1980.

Krug, E. A. *The Shaping of the American High School*. New York: HarperCollins, 1964.

Murphy, M. *Blackboard Unions: The AFT and the NEA: 1900–1980*. Ithaca, N.Y.: Cornell University Press, 1990.

Noble, D. F. *America by Design: Science, Technology and the Rise of Corporate Capitalism*. New York: Knopf, 1979.

Powell, A. G. *The Uncertain Profession: Harvard and the Search for Educational Authority*. Cambridge, England: Cambridge University Press, 1980.

Storr, R. J. *Harper's University: The Beginnings*. Chicago: University of Chicago Press, 1966.

Tyack, D. B. *The One Best System: A History of American Urban Education*. Cambridge, Mass.: Harvard University Press, 1974.

Veysey, L. R. *The Emergence of the American University*. Chicago: University of Chicago Press, 1965.

Wesley, E. B. *NEA: The First Hundred Years*. New York: HarperCollins, 1957.

Whittemore, R. *Nicholas Murray Butler and Public Education: 1862–1911*. New York: Teachers College Press, 1970.

Wiebe, R. H. *The Search for Order, 1877–1920*. New York: Hill and Wang, 1967.

Chapter Three

The Role of State Policy Systems in Fostering Separation or Collaboration

Patrick M. Callan

The responsibility for public policy regarding both the public schools and the public colleges and universities resides primarily at the state level. Governors and legislators are not only the source of public policy, but they are the only entities whose interest, responsibility and authority span public education from preschool through graduate education. Each state's political leadership is responsible for policies that stimulate and require schools and colleges to cooperate in ways that improve student learning, thereby assuring an educated citizenry and a productive workforce, and supporting educational and economic opportunity. But the states' best intentions are frustrated by policy structures and processes that reflect the past, not the future. New links must be forged between the public schools and the colleges; standards for student performance are needed, ones that span the gap between the senior year in high school and the freshman year in college; school reform and teacher education must be linked in planning and implementation; and access to higher education must be maintained as a high priority.

A Short History of a Friendly Divorce

The current state policy framework is rooted in the history of public education in the twentieth century or, more specifically, in the separate histories of the public schools and of public higher education. In the public schools, a dramatic increase in high school enrollment and participation occurred in the first half of the twentieth century. In the colleges and universities, a parallel increase in access and participation took place in the second half of the century. During these periods of intense growth, each system became more complex and purposes became more diffuse. For example, as high schools served an increasingly large portion of American youth in the first half of the century, there were many more high school graduates than those proceeding on to college. Vocational education became increasingly prominent. As colleges grew, they broadened their offerings to meet the educational and training needs of an adult population, not just recent high school graduates.

Over the past fifty years, the earlier, formal ties between the public schools and the colleges were severed. This separation was caused partly by growing complexity and mission differentiation, but it also reflected the aspirations of leaders of schools and colleges that were, in large part, supported by state policy. Research universities established and expanded a dominant knowledge-production paradigm. Normal schools and teachers' colleges were transformed into comprehensive, state universities. As their academic missions broadened, these institutions vainly pursued the research "rabbit." They usually retained the role of training teachers, but providing service to schools, now only one of many functions, lost its priority. Their leaders in teacher education were increasingly drawn from the ranks of disciplinary faculty rather than from those with strong ties to the public schools. In most states, community colleges, which had initially been established by school districts, separated organizationally from the public schools, and the flagship state universities withdrew from examination and accreditation of secondary schools, ceding this function to regional accrediting associations. These developments strengthened the distinctions and built new fences at the boundaries between schools and college. The organizational breaks in the sequential educational process were supported and ratified by state public policies (Brubacher and Rudy, 1958; Dunham, 1969).

Today, we do not need to reinstate the formal mechanisms of governance and administration that once placed schools and colleges under the same administrative structures and boards; these served their purpose and are now history. The linkages that are now urgently needed arise from the imperatives of a new century that will be characterized by technological advance, competition in a world market, and the changing composition of America's youth. Higher standards for student learning and academic achievement, consistently enacted and enforced at every level, are essential if the nation is to retain its democratic character and its high standard of living for all of its citizens.

For more than a decade, various types of collaborative arrangements between schools and colleges have proliferated rapidly. Most programs are initiated and supported locally, but others are statewide and state supported. Many of these arrangements provide financial support and human resources to schools and teachers for outreach and support services to minority and low-income students. The state policy interest both encompasses and transcends these forms of mainly local assistance to schools and students. For as helpful as these programs can be to their direct beneficiaries, they seldom reach the major institutional issues of school reform.

The colleges and universities have not, to say the least, been a major force in the school reform "movements" of the last decade and a half. They have participated to the extent that the reforms were compatible with their own traditions and conventional practices—for example, increasing the Carnegie units required for admission—and when they could support reform on their own terms. Whether justified or not, colleges and universities have often laid the responsibility for their own quality problems—for example, low rates of retention and graduation—at the doorsteps of the public schools. The time has come when higher education must recognize its own responsibilities and do more than complain of ill-prepared high school graduates and grudgingly "back and fill" with remedial courses.

Higher education must acknowledge its responsibility because it holds a near monopoly on critical resources that are essential to improving student achievement in the schools. The colleges and universities determine college admissions requirements; they heavily influence state teacher certification policies; and their faculty have the academic, disciplinary expertise that is rare in the public school hierarchy. It is highly unlikely that significant school reform can occur without the participation of colleges and universities. There are instances of collaboration, but most of these are local and often dependent on problematic grants or contracts, not core funding. Only state policymakers—governors and legislative leaders—can foster collaboration of the breadth and depth that will be required in the new century. Only they have the authority to span the now divided levels of public education. Only they can set statewide agendas, provide fiscal and other incentives for collaboration, and hold both public schools and colleges accountable for building the organizational bridges that are sorely needed.

From Intensification to Standards-Based Reform

Some observers trace the origins of the current, national school reform "movement" to the concerns over the declining SAT scores in the late 1970s; others to the publication of *A Nation at Risk*, the report of the National Commission on Excellence in Education (1983); still others to the passage of the first major state school reform bills. The precipitating event, if there was one, is less important than the remarkably similar patterns of reform that have emerged across the country, patterns that incorporated the general thrust of the recommendations of the National Commission. As school reform evolved in the 1980s and 1990s, these patterns had implications for the three-way relationships among state governments, public schools, and the colleges and universities.

The major point of all these reforms was academic rigor. As one state legislator reportedly put it, "We need to make the little buggers work harder" (Kirst, 1988, p. 320). Indeed, these reforms have been commonly described as "intensification strategies." In the new reforms, the states took greater control of the high school curriculum and adopted new graduation requirements, most often in the areas of English, social studies, mathematics, and science. Statewide assessment tests—a major development of the 1970s—were legislatively established and then extended to additional grade levels and subjects. The state tests, designed primarily to assess minimum competencies, were used for various purposes, including accountability, graduation, and promotion. Other reforms adopted by states included more instructional time, no-pass/no-play rules for student athletes, more homework, and stricter enforcement of discipline and attendance policies.

Colleges and universities usually supported requirements for additional academic courses. Many public four-year colleges and universities, with state encouragement, followed the new high school graduation requirements with more demanding admissions requirements. Although most states do not set admissions policies directly, several—including Florida, Illinois, Oregon, and Wisconsin—for the first time prescribed minimum requirements for freshmen enrolling in public baccalaureate programs. The new requirements, whether established by states or colleges, followed the intensification strategy, typically requiring a college preparatory curriculum and specifying the number of courses in the traditional pattern—English, mathematics, science, social studies—along with minimum grade point averages and required SAT or ACT examination scores (Educational Testing Service, 1990; Massell, Fuhrman, and Associates, 1994).

In adopting their versions of the intensification strategies, colleges and universities took their lead from the state reforms. Implementation of higher entrance requirements did not require either innovation or collaboration on their part. On the contrary, their support was compatible with the prerogative of most colleges and universities to control their admissions policies, and implementation relied on traditional and accepted methods of improving the academic quality of the freshman class. Some colleges may have contributed to intensification by "signaling" to students, parents, and schools the imperative of greater academic preparation for admission to higher education.

The response of the public schools and high school students to the curricular reforms and entrance requirements was one of almost immediate compliance. Although few states fully implemented the curricular recommendations of *A Nation at Risk,* the number of both college-bound students and others taking academic courses increased significantly. For example, Connecticut's high school graduating class of 1988 exceeded the class of 1984 by a third in the proportion of graduates who had taken social science and mathematics classes (Massell, Fuhrman, and Associates, 1994, p. 3). In California, the California State University adopted the University of California's course requirements—the college preparatory sequence known as the "A through F" courses. Between 1985 and 1992, the proportion of California high school graduates completing these courses rose from one-fourth to one-third of the graduating class (Callan and Kirst, 1995). In most states and for the nation, as the number of students taking academic courses increased, so did the number taking the SAT and Advanced Placement examinations.

Despite these signs of progress, other indicators suggested that the intensification strategies were not producing the gains in actual student learning that had been anticipated. Student scores on the National Assessment of Educational Progress (NAEP) showed little progress between 1980 and 1990. As measured by NAEP, student achievement from the beginning to the end of the 1980s was summarized as follows (Educational Testing Service, 1990, p. 27):

Reading. There were no gains in average proficiency in the 1980s.

Mathematics. There was some improvement in average proficiency in the 1980s; however, there was essentially none at the higher level we associate with having taken several years of high school math.

Science. The U.S. has been bringing up the rear in science achievement among countries of the developed world. From this low level of achievement, improvement began in the 1980s at all three levels assessed by NAEP.

Civics. There was basically no improvement in civics knowledge
in the 1980s, and some ground was lost among 17-year-olds.

Writing. Our students are poor writers and they're not improving. . . . There was no progress in the 1980s.

Few states track individual student performance from high
school through college, so very little is known about the impact of
the high school graduation and college admission policies as students cross the structural gap. Studies from Illinois and Oklahoma
did show higher ACT scores and improved performance and
higher retention rates in the freshman year (Rodriguez, 1995).
Anecdotal information from colleges and universities and from
national and regional studies, however, revealed that taking more
rigorous, academic, high school courses had not reduced the need
for remedial college courses. The National Center for Education
Statistics (1994) reported that approximately 30 percent of first-
time freshmen were enrolled in a remedial reading, mathematics,
or writing course in the fall of 1989. According to the Southern
Regional Education Board (1991), over 35 percent of freshmen in
the South were enrolled in remedial courses. An American Council on Education profile of undergraduates, relying on student-
reported information, found that 13 percent of all undergraduates,
mostly freshmen, took at least one remedial course in 1992–1993
(Knopp, 1996). In the early and mid-1990s, remedial education
became a volatile issue within higher education, often reaching the
governing board level, and in some instances becoming both an
educational and fiscal concern of state legislatures and the media.

In sum, colleges and universities participated in the intensification phase of the early and mid-1980s by supporting state curricular mandates with their own mandates in the form of new
admissions policies. As disappointing as the results of these reforms
may have been, the sea change in course-taking patterns of American high school students in the late 1980s and early 1990s demonstrates the profound influence that colleges can have on schools,
particularly when school reform and college admission policies are
compatible.

Amid the mounting evidence that the intensification strategies had not produced major gains in student learning, leaders in public school reform began to move away from the highly prescriptive regulation of school inputs and procedures derived from *A Nation at Risk*. The second generation of school reforms shifted emphasis to educational results—that is, to defining and assessing student learning achievement. This emphasis called for developing an "infrastructure" of policy instruments, including curriculum frameworks that specified high standards. It required providing assessments to measure learning against standards, and giving discretion to schools and professional educators at the school sites for learning strategies that would reach the standards. As the states and the schools move to standards-based reform, one major question is whether colleges and universities will come to the table as participants in developing standards and in reshaping their admissions policies to support standards-based reform.

Colleges and universities could participate relatively easily in the initial efforts at reform because the intensification approaches relied on upgrading the conventional tools of college admissions— that is, grade point averages, broad tests of college readiness such as the SAT and ACT examinations, and Carnegie units. In contrast, standards-based admissions policy would require substantial revision of college admissions practices. Traditional reliance on course requirements and general tests would give way to specifying and assessing the knowledge and skills needed for college-level work. College admissions would emphasize content, and leave the structure of the curriculum to the schools. Explicit content standards would send clear signals to the schools about what students must know and be able to do in college.

Standards-based admissions policies would require significant collaboration among colleges and universities to identify new admissions criteria and to communicate clearly with schools and students. Such policies would also demand more collaborative relationships with schools than in the past to assure consistency in the knowledge and skills expected of students. Most fundamentally, the new approach would require colleges and universities to relinquish their traditional prerogative and responsibility of dictating the specific high school curriculum of college-bound students. Colleges would also begin to modify their own courses—in content and presentation—to take account of what their incoming students have learned and how they learned it.

If state colleges and schools operate at cross-purposes, the promise held out by standards-based reform is not likely to be realized. Many colleges and university leaders are seriously skeptical about new approaches to admissions. Despite the stark reality that the significantly increased number of students taking academic courses has not made a major dent in the need for remediation, many college leaders are predisposed either to continue down that path, hoping for future gains, or to assume a "wait and see" approach to standards-based reform. Large public institutions and systems, in particular, are wary of the administrative, financial, and political implications of modifying or replacing the standardized, quantitative measures currently used for ranking and admitting candidates (Haughton, 1993). The current controversy over affirmative action in college admissions may have made some college leaders and admissions officers even more reluctant to depart from conventional—even mechanistic—admissions practices.

State policy leadership is needed to bring secondary and higher education leaders together in a search for common ground. This process is under way in several states, including Oregon, Wisconsin, and Colorado. The Oregon Proficiency-Based Admissions Policy (PASS) appears to be the most ambitious effort. It is being designed to align admissions policies with performance measures for public education, and to specify and assess the knowledge and skills needed to benefit from college instruction. The program is to be fully implemented by 2002. Other states may experiment with performance-based admissions alternatives while, in the short term, maintaining the conventional systems. For every state, a debate on the standards-based school reform and college admissions would bring state, public school, and higher education leaders together in a deepened conversation about student learning, its improvement and evaluation.

Teacher Preparation

The preparation of teachers is one of the most direct ways colleges and universities influence the quality of public school education. State governments control the program accreditation and teacher credentialing processes. And schools provide the student teaching experience for teacher trainees. In the state reform legislation of the 1980s, teacher education was the subject of its own intensification strategy aimed primarily at raising the quality of teachers. Most states enacted tests of basic skills and minimum competencies for entry into the teaching profession, certification, or both. In addition, a number of states revised their state requirements for teacher education programs. These changes invariably placed greater emphasis on preparation in the academic disciplines and reduced emphasis on pedagogy (Educational Testing Service, 1990, pp. 8, 9).

Notwithstanding this flurry of legislation, the findings of a series of reports and studies in the early 1990s were highly critical of the state of teacher education. Among the major criticisms were that the education of teachers was disconnected from the schools and from the reforms that were intended to reshape the schools; that the teacher education programs were a low priority of colleges, and even of schools of education; and that these programs were cumbersome and over-regulated by states. A series of interviews with 150 state legislators, governors' staffs, and state agency leaders by the Education Commission of the States (ECS) found "a remarkable agreement on the ineffectiveness of the current system," and summarized the perspectives of many legislators and governors: "Public schools struggling with restructuring cannot be handicapped each year with the arrival of thousands of new teachers unprepared to respond to the public demand for change." The proposed solutions of most state leaders were characterized in the ECS report as "a disturbing willingness to grasp at a single solution" (Frazier, 1993, pp. 1, 4).

Despite the negative evaluations and the frustrations of governmental leaders, there was considerable convergence of themes among the organized proponents of reform, including the Holmes Group, the Renaissance Group, and John Goodlad in his major study of teacher education (Holmes Group, 1986, 1989; Renaissance Group, 1989; Goodlad, 1990). These groups recommended strengthening the role of arts and sciences faculty in teacher preparation, and building links between them and the schools of education. They recommended establishing "professional development schools" to link higher education and public school faculty for collaborative improvement of the clinical component of teacher preparation and school reform. Other program modifications included lengthening the programs beyond four years. With the exception of calls for reducing or eliminating prescriptive state regulations, however, the reform reports did not call for state government to take an active, leading role in reforming teacher education.

The reluctance of education reformers to call for state leadership in an area of policy that has been characterized by state micromanagement of curricula, courses, and time is understandable. Elimination of highly prescriptive and detailed state regulation of teacher education may be a necessary condition for implementation of reforms, but it is not likely to be sufficient. And state passivity is not likely to hasten change.

There are several major steps that state policymakers should take to stimulate and hasten the pace of reform of teacher education. States could agree to deregulate teacher education and substitute rigorous assessment of the knowledge and skills of candidates for teacher credentials. Such assessments would include basic skills, subject matter expertise, pedagogical theory, and teaching practice. The purpose would be to create a licensure process for individual teachers parallel to that for other professions. (The Interstate New

Teacher Assessment and Support Consortium, under the auspices of the Council of Chief State School Officers, is developing model standards for initial teacher licensure in a collaborative effort of several professional associations and seventeen states [Interstate New Teacher Assessment and Support Consortium, 1992, pp. 1–11].) The development of standards and assessments should be a joint responsibility of college and school leaders. Collaboration would assure that changes in teacher education are jointly planned and implemented.

States should also consider a special, state funding mechanism for clinical or professional development schools. Special funding would be an incentive for collaboration and would recognize that some additional costs are inherent in the idea, which is labor intensive for both school and college faculties. The state funds might be fully or partially matched by school districts and colleges. If special funding is made available, the state should require that schools and colleges apply jointly for support.

Early in his study of teacher education, John Goodlad noted that "during successive eras of education reform, the reform of schools and the reform of teacher education have rarely been connected" (Goodlad, 1990, p. 3). State policy leadership may be required to make that critical connection. Only the state can eliminate regulatory burdens, stimulate the collaborative redesign of teacher education programs by schools and colleges, require the development of assessments of the competencies of prospective teachers against explicit standards, and provide incentives for professional development schools.

Access to Higher Education

Journalist Nicholas Lemann recently observed that "access to college is not an abstract, faraway, dreamy issue to most Americans. It is the crucial point around which they orient their lives as they raise their children" (1996, p. 38). While this may not yet be true for the most disadvantaged Americans, the opportunity for college is the single most powerful motivation and achievement at the pre-collegiate levels of schooling. States have the primary responsibility for providing educational opportunity beyond high school. Most of the increase in access and participation in American higher education has occurred because of expansion of public higher education by the states. Now is the time to assure that access remains available to the coming generation, a generation that in many states will be very different in ethnicity and financial resources than today's students.

After a half-century of broadened college opportunity, increased demand and constrained financial resources are casting a shadow over the accessibility of college for the coming cohorts of high school students. The nation's high school graduating classes will increase dramatically over the next fifteen years. These students are already born and making their way through the nation's elementary and secondary schools. By the year 2009, the number of high school graduates is projected to increase by 32 percent over the number in 1992. The graduating class of 2008 will be 3.3 million, exceeding that of 1979, the peak year of baby-boom high school graduates. There are significant regional and state variations within this broad national picture. Some states, such as Louisiana, Wyoming, North Dakota, and Maine, will experience declines in high school graduates, while such states as Nevada, California, and Florida will experience dramatic increases—over 200 percent, 50 percent, and 70 percent, respectively. In addition, the next cohorts of high school graduates will reflect the demographic shifts in the American population. Young Americans are more ethnically heterogeneous. This is particularly true in states that will experience the greatest growth in numbers of high school graduates (Western Interstate Commission for Higher Education, Teachers Insurance and Annuity Association, and The College Board, 1993; Breneman, Estrada, and Hayward, 1995).

Dubbed "Tidal Wave II" by Clark Kerr (1994, p. 2), these increases in high school graduates will bring greater demand for college opportunity than at any time since the tidal wave of baby boomers reached college age in the 1960s and 1970s. These next generations of college-age students will test the commitment of the states to educational opportunity, a public policy commitment that has been assumed for three decades. In contrast to the expansionist era of the baby boomers, they will knock on college doors at a time of severely constrained public financial resources. State resources will be scarce, regardless of recovery from the recent recession; health care, welfare, and corrections will be strong competitors for state dollars.

There are many reasons—economic, social, civic, and educational—states should maintain and enhance accessible, affordable systems of higher education. Among them is the message that college opportunity sends to young people, their families, and the schools: that college opportunity is there for those who work hard, complete high school, and achieve at high levels. States that limit accessibility will also lag in their economic development, as industries search relentlessly for highly educated workforces. If states, by design or by indirection, support or accept the erosion or reduction of postsecondary educational opportunity, they will undermine their own efforts to reform schools and to foster school-college collaboration as a means to that end.

Conclusion

Accessible higher education is an essential component, often overlooked, in policy strategies for improving student learning in the schools. Without collaboration across the boundary between the two sectors, the public schools are unlikely to discover and use adequate measures of student progress; the colleges are unlikely to educate effective teachers; and the aspirations for providing quality public education cannot be fully realized by either the states, the public schools, or the colleges.

The overarching role of state government is too often overlooked as the public schools and the colleges and universities wrestle with problems in isolation from one another. Admittedly, each sector's experience with governmental micro-management and bureaucratic red tape discourages appeals to the ultimate authority of the state, but many governors and legislatures are learning that not all wisdom resides in Albany or Sacramento. Locally, some schools and colleges are effectively spanning the gap between secondary and higher education, and these examples must be preserved. The fact remains, however, that a significant policy bridge between the public schools and the colleges can only be built in state capitols. The public schools cannot meet the demands of the new century by going it alone; neither can the colleges and universities. The state must participate as an active player to encourage—probably require—collaboration. This may sometimes require "head-knocking" of competitive, sometimes hostile state agencies and interest groups that have long been separate. At the same time, the state must also leave enough play in the joints so that the educational machine will run. Some new state funding will be needed, but if that funding is strategically invested, the costs of building new connections and capacities need not be overwhelming. Each state must find its own route to the future of its schools and colleges, but the dawning of wisdom lies in realizing that both sectors comprise a single system.

References

Breneman, D. W., Estrada, L. F., and Hayward, G. C. *Tidal Wave II: An Evaluation of Enrollment Projections*. San Jose: California Higher Education Policy Center, 1995.

Brubacher, J., and Rudy, W. *Higher Education in Transition: An American History, 1636–1956*. New York: HarperCollins, 1958.

Callan, P. M., and Kirst, M. W. "Promises Unkept: The Crisis in Higher Education Enrollment." *California Schools*, 1995, 54(2).

Dunham, E. A. *Colleges of the Forgotten Americans: A Profile of State Colleges and Regional Universities*. New York: McGraw-Hill, 1969.

Educational Testing Service. *The Education Reform Decade*. Princeton, N.J.: Educational Testing Service, 1990.

Frazier, C. F. *A Shared Vision: Policy Recommendations for Linking Teacher Education to School Reform*. Denver: Education Commission of the States, 1993.

Goodlad, J. I. *Teachers for Our Nation's Schools*. San Francisco: Jossey-Bass, 1990.

Haughton, M. J. *College Admissions Standards and School Reform: Toward a Partnership in Education*. Washington, D.C.: National Governors' Association, 1993.

Holmes Group. *Tomorrow's Teachers: A Report of the Holmes Group*. East Lansing, Mich.: Holmes Group, 1986.

Holmes Group. *Work in Progress: The Holmes Group One Year On*. East Lansing, Mich.: Holmes Group, 1989.

Interstate New Teacher Assessment and Support Consortium. *Model Standards for Beginning Teacher Licensure and Development*. Washington, D.C.: Council of Chief State School Officers, 1992.

Kerr, C. *Preserving the Master Plan*. San Jose: California Higher Education Policy Center, 1994.

Kirst, M. W. "Recent State Education Reform in the United States: Looking Forward and Backward." *Education Administration Quarterly*, 1988, *24*, 319–328.

Knopp, L. "Remedial Education: An Undergraduate Student Profile." *American Council on Education Research Briefs*, 1996, 6(8).

Lemann, N. "Open the Doors to College." *Washington Monthly*, 1996, 28(1, 2), 38–39.

Massell, D., Fuhrman, S., and Associates. *Ten Years of State Education Reform, 1983–1993: Overview with Four Case Studies*. New Brunswick, N.J.: Rutgers University, and Madison, Wis.: Consortium for Policy Research in Education, 1994.

National Center for Education Statistics. "College-Level Remedial Education in the Fall of 1989." Washington, D.C.: U.S. Government Printing Office, 1994.

National Commission on Excellence in Education. *A Nation at Risk*. Washington, D.C.: National Commission on Excellence in Education, 1983.

Renaissance Group. *Teachers for the New World: A Statement of Principles*. Cedar Falls: University of Northern Iowa, 1989.

Rodriguez, E. M. *College Admissions Requirements: A New Role for States*. Denver: State Higher Education Executive Officers and the Education Commission of the States, 1995.

Southern Regional Education Board. *They Came to College? A Remedial Developmental Profile of First-Time Freshmen in the SREB States*. Atlanta: Southern Regional Education Board, 1991.

Western Interstate Commission for Higher Education, Teachers Insurance and Annuity Association, and The College Board. *High School Graduates: Projections by State, 1992–2009*. Boulder, Colo.: Western Interstate Commission for Higher Education, Teachers Insurance and Annuity Association, and The College Board, 1993.

Chapter Four

School-College Partnerships

Kati Haycock

Around the turn of the century, leaders in higher education were much concerned about quality and variability in secondary education. Indeed, complaints from academicians then were hardly different from those heard on college campuses today.

Earlier college and university leaders acted on their worries in a manner quite different from that of today's leaders, however. During the last decade of the nineteenth century and the first decade of the twentieth century, higher education leaders joined together on a series of occasions to take bold steps to shape much of secondary education. Acting under various banners—including that of the National Education Association—they dictated a college preparatory curriculum, established units (Carnegie units and semesters) for measuring curricular coverage, created accrediting associations to inspect school quality, and set up a testing association in an effort to control for school variability (Brubacher and Rudy, 1958). By all accounts, these measures were designed to affect secondary education as a whole; they were even "aligned" in much the same manner as advocated by today's advocates of "systemic" reform; and they did have pronounced, long-term effects on schools and the students who attended them.

By contrast, today's college and university leaders have rejected big levers in favor of small, people-to-people programs. With precious few exceptions, they have explicitly refused to take the bold steps that are available to them if they act collectively—like raising admissions requirements, reinvigorating accreditation mechanisms, or transforming teacher preparation. Instead, colleges and universities provided a launching pad for a vibrant movement to bring pre-collegiate teachers and students together with college faculty and students in ways that will enhance educational quality and opportunity.

Today, there are thousands of such partnerships. They involve every kind of higher education institution—community colleges, liberal arts institutions, comprehensive institutions, and research universities. Current partnerships tend to be less uni-directional than the traditional ways in which colleges and universities relate to schools, and they are more likely to involve traditional academic departments than schools of education (Wilbur and Lambert, 1995). Though large in number, these partnerships tend to serve relatively small numbers of students or professionals; the typical partnership today links one college with fewer than ten schools. As such, the effects of this generation of higher education initiatives, though often quite wonderful for participating teachers and students, may be more marginal than those of the previous era.

In this chapter I examine three "waves" of school-college partnerships launched during the past three decades. I also explore the apparent mismatch between higher education's current ad hoc strategy and the movement toward "systemic" reform under way in K–12. I conclude by describing a newer wave of collaborative activity, sometimes called "K–16 reform," that seeks to combine the bolder leverage strategies from earlier times with the helping strategies from the partnerships era to produce higher-quality schools and colleges, and by outlining some of the key tasks for higher education in systemic reform.

The First Wave of Partnership Programs: 1965–Present

The first wave of school-college partnerships got under way during the late 1960s and early 1970s when colleges and universities came under increasing pressure to increase the number of minority students enrolling at the undergraduate level. Most responded in the way that made sense to them: Create a new "minority outreach program," hire recruiters and assign them to go out and find minority students.

This strategy did produce gains, but its limits soon became apparent. At the time, both black and Latino students were graduating from high school at rates considerably below those of Anglo students. Moreover, disproportionately few of those who did graduate had completed a college preparatory curriculum (often because their high school counselors had "tracked" them into the general or vocational curriculum, but sometimes because their high school lacked a credible version of such a preparatory curriculum). Such students could, of course, be admitted anyway (and thousands were), but poor preparation would make it difficult for them to succeed.

Clearly, if colleges and universities were to succeed in diversifying their enrollments, they needed to find ways to improve this situation. Given that the young people to whom they wanted access were most often found in schools, college officials would need the cooperation of school people to reach them.

Though they were often named with words like *partnership*—at least in part to obtain the necessary cooperation—the programs launched during this period were usually collaborative in name only. They were driven almost entirely by higher education employees, many of whom were deeply suspicious of the motivations of their counterparts in K–12. During this time, higher education staff looked to colleagues in K–12 only for access to students; in the main, they did not see them as a source of information or guidance.

Institutions of higher education launched two basic types of programs during this period: informational and preparatory. The first type sought to identify promising minority students before the senior year in high school and to acquaint them with college opportunities and requirements. Often, the college employees who staffed these programs were from the same ethnic groups as the targeted students, and they formed close bonds with the students over time.

The second type of program was intended to provide enriched academic experiences for promising minority students whose schools were not providing sufficiently rigorous preparation for college. Often held after school, on Saturdays, or during the summer months, these programs brought minority students onto college campuses for special classes in math, science, writing, or study skills. Graduates from the programs would then be admitted and provided, usually, with extra financial aid.

Some of these programs were financed with institutional resources or state dollars. The University of California, one of the first into this arena, launched its Educational Opportunity Program in the early 1960s with support from the UC Regents' "Opportunity Funds." For many colleges and universities, however, Title IV of the Higher Education Act of 1965 became the principal source of support for new programs to encourage college enrollment. Title IV authorizes the federal TRIO programs, which now include Upward Bound, Talent Search, Educational Opportunity Centers, Student Support Services, and Early Intervention Partnerships. The federal government appropriated approximately $450 million for these programs in 1995.

The Second Wave of Partnership Programs: 1980–Present

The second wave of school-college partnership activity got under way in the 1980s, in the aftermath of *A Nation at Risk* (National Commission on Excellence in Education, 1983). Unlike the first wave of activity, which was motivated by concerns about equity and focused directly on students, this group of programs was motivated by concerns about quality, and aimed at helping teachers to achieve teaching excellence.

Many of the new programs were based loosely on the model of the Bay Area Writing Project, a UC Berkeley–based program to help good writing teachers become better writers and better teachers of writing. The core idea was a "teachers-teaching-teachers" or "trainer-of-trainers" approach, wherein graduates of an intensive summer program would return to their school to help their peers improve the teaching of (in this example) writing. During the 1980s, the Writing Project swept the nation.

There was much activity in other disciplines, as well. During the mid-1980s, Claire Gaudiani, then University of Pennsylvania professor and now Connecticut College president, led a national effort to spawn "Academic Alliances," organizations that brought college faculty members together on a regular basis with K–12 teachers in the same discipline to discuss developments in the field, share teaching strategies, and so on. There are now more than 500 such alliances across the country, most of them organized quite informally and operating on shoestring budgets.

From the beginning, college faculty members in math and science fields have been especially energetic in forming and conducting partnerships. Funding has been plentiful in these disciplines, as well, with generous investments through the National Science Foundation (NSF) and the federal Eisenhower Professional Development Program, as well as from private corporations and foundations. Math and science are the areas, too, where the impulses behind the two "waves" of partnership activity—equity and excellence—are most regularly joined.

By the late 1980s, almost every college and university in the country served as home to teacher-oriented programs in a host of disciplines. In the history department on a typical college campus, one faculty member might have been working to help twenty high school teachers from a local school district incorporate original materials into their teaching strategies, while another might have been working with fifteen elementary teachers to infuse geography into their history lessons. Meanwhile, across the campus, two mathematicians might have teamed up to start a "Math Project" (similar to the Writing Project) to help math teachers learn how to incorporate manipulatives into their teaching, while a professor in computer science helped teachers in a nearby school make selections from available hardware and software.

Second-wave partnership programs are almost always initiated by individuals within higher education, usually faculty members who are concerned enough to get involved with local teachers even though the work is seldom recognized or rewarded on the college campus. As might be expected, these programs tend to be run more collaboratively than the equity programs. In fact, while typically based on a college campus, some of the very best of these programs are actually governed by teachers. This does not mean, however, that they consistently are aligned with the reform plans and activities of a school district or state education agency. Indeed, more often they are not.

The Third Wave of Partnership Programs: 1990–Present

The newest wave of partnership activity is focused on preparing students for the workplace. Most often, these new programs join high schools and community colleges, but some include four-year colleges, as well. They also involve a new partner: business. A recent national survey of partnership activity found faster growth in the "vocational-technical" field than any other (Wilbur and Lambert, 1995).

Most of these partnerships were forged after 1990, when the federal Perkins Vocational Education Act was reauthorized. This act directed dollars toward the development and operation of "tech prep" or "2 + 2" programs, which combine a focused vocational program during the last two years of high school with two years of vocational training at the community college level. When President Clinton signed the School to Work Opportunities Act into law in 1994, there was another surge of collaborative activity in this field. Basically, the School to Work Act envisions a connected system in which high school–age students—including those who are college bound—receive preparation for the workplace while they are still in high school. That training would typically be deepened later, either in an apprenticeship or in a vocationally oriented postsecondary program.

At both the local and statewide levels, community colleges have been actively involved in the development of expanded school-to-work initiatives; indeed, they are often involved as campuses, rather than simply as a handful of interested faculty members. Employers are also heavily involved. To date, though, most four-year institutions have not become actively involved in program design and implementation—some because they perceive "school to work" to be exactly what it says and others because the vocational focus of these programs seems incompatible with their own liberal arts curricula.

School-College Partnerships: Where Are We Today?

There is no accurate count of the number of school-college partnerships in existence today, but the evidence points to numbers in the many thousands. In the second edition of *Linking America's Schools and Colleges* (1995), for example, Franklin Wilbur and Leo Lambert report data on some 2,200 partnerships unearthed in a survey of 2,600 chief academic officers. An earlier report from the National Association of Independent Colleges and Universities described more than a thousand such programs in private colleges and universities alone. Other inventories compiled by campus presidents or state system chancellors often run to hundreds of pages.

The numbers appear to be growing—and not always in ways that one might predict. For example, given the tremendous pressure on K–12 teachers to improve student performance measured against new academic standards, one might have predicted a shift from student-focused programming to professional development partnerships in the various academic disciplines. Indeed, the most recent survey does report growth in the number of professional development partnerships over the past five years, from a growth rate of 22 percent in writing/English to 63 percent in the social sciences. Over the five-year period, however, professional development initiatives dropped from 32.6 percent of all reported partnership programs to 29 percent, while student-focused partnerships grew from 42.9 to 51.6 percent of the whole (Wilbur and Lambert, 1995).

Another surprise—and one that bears careful watching—is how many partnerships report start-dates after 1990: in the current volume, 1000 of the 2200 partnerships. Although this may be in part an artifact of the particular survey approach employed, and in part a reflection of the current growth spurt in partnership activity, it could also suggest that much partnership activity is short-lived. This may be a function of the paucity of external financial support (nearly half of all partnerships receive no outside financial support) or the lack of internal rewards for faculty participating in partnership activity. Because we know that school teachers and students need consistent support over a period of years, this phenomenon is problematic.

Given the state of the support system for collaborative activity, it is amazing how vibrant and vigorous this partnerships movement is. Participants on all sides—school teachers, students, and college faculty—report that these activities are among those that they value the most. Teachers talk about the self-esteem and sense of professionalism that flow from being treated as colleagues by faculty in research universities; students talk about the new confidence that comes from successful work in enrichment courses taught by college faculty; and college faculty frequently report a new interest in their own teaching and in learning more about how students learn. Conferences on collaboration, including the American Association for Higher Education's National Conference on School/College Collaboration and the annual conference of the National Alliance for Partnerships in Education, draw large crowds of both long-time and new collaborators looking for ideas on how to improve the effectiveness of their work.

Perhaps most important of all, the people who work in school-college partnerships increasingly see themselves as part of a single profession and a single system of education, from kindergarten through college. They tend to view the challenges of today's classrooms as a shared responsibility, and have formed relationships based on shared goals. As Wilbur and Lambert point out in their introduction to *Linking America's Schools and Colleges* (1995), the most important contribution of this partnership movement could be a "transformed education profession."

The Impact of Partnership Programs

Given the investments of time and resources in partnership programs, we should know considerably more than we do about their impact on what is important: student achievement. After all, it was the underachievement of minority students that gave rise to the first wave of these programs, the underachievement of American students more generally that gave rise to the second wave, and the lack of preparation for work that gave rise to the third wave. Have these programs made a difference?

Most of the more formal programs have undergone at least some evaluation. Interestingly, though, the emphasis within these evaluations has almost always been on *service* provided. So we know, for example, how many students participated in the "College Bounders Club," how many attended Saturday or after school sessions, how many participated in the summer session, and (sometimes) how many enrolled in College X. But we rarely know how many would have enrolled in College X anyway, how the students actually fared in the college, how many went elsewhere, how many would have gone elsewhere anyway, and so on. Basically, little control group evaluation has been undertaken in this arena. The limited evidence we have seems to suggest that most of these interventions are insufficient to make a long-term difference.

The evaluations on the teacher-oriented programs are no better. Despite their original inspiration, most of these programs focused on "increasing teacher professionalism," not on improving student achievement. Many project directors actively resisted efforts to evaluate the impact on student learning; their assessments of impact on classroom practice were also not very thorough. The few careful evaluations of this type of professional development, however, raise grave questions about the effectiveness of programs that do not provide long-term support, observation, and coaching back in the classroom—and most campus-based programs do not. Such evaluations also raise questions about the trainer-of-trainers model, without a more comprehensive organizational change effort in the school or school district as a whole.

In the tech-prep or school-to-work arena, most programs are too new to have had much evaluation. The research seems to suggest a mixed picture. Some, like the "Academies" model developed in Northern California, appear to succeed with students who have little success in other programs. Others appear to contribute little to the employability of their graduates.

Because of the limited research base, it is difficult to draw conclusions about the contributions of collaborative programs to the educational bottom line: student achievement. In the end, we are probably left with more basic questions: Are we concerned about low levels of literacy and numeracy reported by the National Assessment of Educational Progress (NAEP), about the apparently large gap in math and science between American students and students in other industrialized nations, and about the still substantial gap that separates low-income and minority students at all levels from other students? If so, are there other ways in which higher education might contribute to improved quality and increased learning?

Systemic Reform

Across the country, leaders in business, government, and K–12 education who are dissatisfied with current levels of achievement have worked hard to develop a strategy to move beyond the few success stories and make whole school systems successful with all of their students. After years of experience with a vague improvement strategy that sought "excellence" but never defined it, these leaders have settled on a strategy called *standards-based systemic reform*. In state after state, government leaders are throwing out old policies—most of which focused on regulation of the inputs and processes of education—and focusing, instead, on student outcomes.

As they work, the reformers are striving to reinvent the rules by which American students are educated—most of which were set by higher education leaders around the turn of the century. They argue, for example, that

- Measuring student progress by a time-based system of accumulating credit hours and Carnegie units should give way to measuring what students know and are able to do
- Instead of simply requiring certain courses of study, educational authorities should examine students for the learning that takes place inside these courses
- Instead of grouping students into "college-" and "non-college-bound" tracks, the demands of modern society suggest that all students should be taught to high standards
- Aptitude tests that cannot be studied for and that have as their purpose the selection of winners should give way to performance assessments that can be studied for and that reward student effort

The old rules, they say, do not make sense for the new century.

Over the past several years, a consensus has been developing on the need for new rules and a systemic approach to education reform. The main idea here is to strive for coherence all the way up and down the line: If we believe that all students can learn to high standards, then we must organize our classrooms and schools around that goal, and reorder district and state policies accordingly.

The change strategy that has emerged from this work—and that is now embodied in the federal Goals: 2000 and Improving America's Schools Acts—has seven elements:

- Establish clear, high goals or standards for what all students should know and be able to do.

- Develop assessments to measure student performance against those standards.

- Vest authority for determining how to get students to the standards in local teachers, administrators, and parents, and create mechanisms to engage them in making the necessary improvements in curriculum and instruction.

- Provide substantial professional and organizational development as educators and others take on new roles.

- Assure that all students have an opportunity to learn to the new standards.

- Hold schools and districts accountable for improving each year the number of their students—including poor and minority students—who meet state standards; provide incentives and rewards for progress and assure change where progress is lacking.

- Report regularly to the larger community about student progress toward the standards.

In short, *standards-based systemic reform* is simply a name for the kind of change strategy that might be launched in any other institution: business, government, or education. Be clear about goals, constantly assess how you are doing, concentrate on changing the processes that produce outcomes, get help when you need it, aim for improvement, and reward progress.

New Roles for Higher Education

So far, higher education has played no significant role either in the development of systemic reform strategies or in their implementation. If that does not change, the movement toward standards-based systemic reform strategies will probably be derailed. Why? There are two main reasons: First, many of the core tasks of systemic reform—for example, developing and aligning content and performance—cannot be carried out well and on sufficient scale without active cooperation from higher education. Second, if higher education clings to old rules as K–12 leaders adopt new ones, teachers, parents, and students will be confused about what is important, and considerable energy will be wasted. This is especially true of admissions requirements, which exert a powerful influence on what is taught in K–12.

Recognizing these problems, K–12 and higher education leaders in more than thirty cities have come together to develop more coherent, coordinated strategies that link the two systems in a coordinated improvement effort. Some have even gone a further step: to admit that higher education, itself, could benefit from a "systemic" reform strategy focused on improving student outcomes, and to begin to develop that strategy. Many of the most ambitious of these "K–16" reform initiatives are funded by the Pew Charitable Trusts through its Community Compacts Initiative.

Brief profiles of some of the work in three such cities follow.

El Paso

In 1992, the University of Texas at El Paso (UTEP) President Diana Natalicio approached the superintendents of the three largest El Paso school districts and the president of the local community college with a simple question: "Are there some things that we can do together that will increase the success of El Paso young people in school and in college?" As president of a regional institution that draws a large share of its students from local high schools, Natalicio knew that her institution's success was in many ways dependent on the success of local school districts in educating their largely poor, Latino student population. Similarly, district leaders knew that, because UTEP produced the lion's share of their teachers and because UTEP's admissions requirements set a target for many students, their success in getting their students to higher levels of achievement was in many ways dependent on the university.

Both sets of leaders were tired of programmatic approaches to improving student success and were anxious to mount a more comprehensive reform effort.

In short order, these leaders agreed to establish a new organization—the El Paso Collaborative for Educational Excellence—that would serve as a vehicle for their collective improvement effort. The Collaborative is governed by a board that includes the CEOs of the three participating school districts and two participating colleges, as well as strong voices from the community, including the lead organizer of the Alinsky-based El Paso Interreligious Sponsoring Organization (EPISO), the head of the chamber of commerce, and the county judge.

El Paso has mounted a multi-pronged reform strategy that includes agreement on clear, high standards for student achievement, development of new assessments to measure progress, support for site-based decision making, and several other "essential elements" of systemic reform. The standards development process they have employed is particularly compelling.

Unlike some reform leaders, who seem to believe that the simple publication of national or state standards will automatically improve student achievement, the leaders in El Paso want teachers at all levels—and, indeed, the community itself—to "own" the standards. They believe that standards simply handed down from on high would be standards ignored.

The El Pasoans also believe that, for the standards to have maximum effect, they must be adopted by both the colleges and the school districts, so that students, teachers, and parents will have a single message about what is important. Consequently, the process began in 1993–1994 with the appointment of committees in each discipline, composed of equal numbers of K–12 and higher education faculty. Their charge was to decide what students needed to know and be able to do in order to graduate from high school and gain admission to higher education.

The following year, the Collaborative Board appointed "writing committees," composed of higher education faculty, teachers, parents, and employers, to draft standards for grades 4, 8, and 12. To assure that these standards aligned with the highest national and international standards, the committees worked not only from the product of the earlier committees but also from the best national and state standards developed elsewhere.

The products of these writing committees then were submitted for detailed review in various community settings, as well as by employers and parents. The latter effort was accomplished with the assistance of EPISO organizers, who held "house meetings" in a variety of low-income neighborhoods to review the drafts with parents.

In May 1996 the product of this work—the El Paso Standards for Academic Excellence—were released to the community as a whole at an event that featured Texas Governor George W. Bush. The Collaborative then turned its energies to helping teachers put the standards to work in classrooms throughout El Paso.

The Collaborative's implementation plans include expansion of an eighteen-month-old Fund for Innovation in Education-financed "standards-based professional development" initiative. Through this initiative, teachers in six schools have been working together, using work from their own students to fashion performance standards and develop appropriate curriculum and assessment tasks. During the school year, participating teachers are released from their teaching activities on at least a biweekly basis to do this work. In the summer, they come together for uninterrupted periods.

The El Paso strategy also includes considerable support for leadership teams from participating schools, including summer institutes where they can assess progress and plan for the future, monthly seminars for principals, and intensive professional development for math and science teachers. In a departure from practice in other cities, where superintendents serve as principal investigators for NSF-funded Urban Systemic Initiatives (USI), the Collaborative director serves as principal investigator for the El Paso USI, coordinating a math and science reform effort that includes more than thirty mentor teachers and costs several million dollars per year.

There are changes under way in higher education, as well. First among these is a complete overhaul of the teacher education program at UTEP, guided by Dean Arturo Pacheco with the advice of teachers from schools participating in the Collaborative's work. Indeed, most of the training now takes place in those schools. One of the other interesting changes involves EPISO organizers, who now help train future teachers and administrators how to involve and organize parents in the communities they serve. Changes are under way, too, in the math and the science departments, where faculty members have been examining student success rates and devising ways to improve them.

In 1996, these improvement efforts were broadened to include departments throughout the University. Each department was asked to decide on its own goals for student learning—for what all of its majors should know and be able to do. Further, each department had to decide how it would assist student learning. Eventually, these "standards" will become the basis for a university-wide accountability system, as well as for efforts to assist faculty members to improve student learning.

Pueblo

Pueblo, Colorado, is one of the most interesting examples of new ways of linking higher education and K–12 because it has joined the two systems formally. In an agreement signed by University of Southern Colorado President Robert Shirley and the leaders of Pueblo School District No. 60, the two institutions combined certain key functions in 1993. Superintendent Henry Roman is now a vice president of the university, and the two institutions have combined their planning, purchasing, facilities management, and print operations—with the resulting savings plowed back into core instruction. They also established a single Center on Teaching and Learning, staffed by both K–12 and higher education faculty and charged with preparing teachers and assisting in the improvement of teaching at both levels. The director of that center is also the deputy superintendent of the school district.

Through its Community Compact, education and community leaders in Pueblo incorporated the community college and neighboring School District No. 70 into a larger improvement effort. The Pueblo Chamber of Commerce and Hispanic Chamber have also been active partners, especially in the standards development process, where they actually rejected a draft document as too fuzzy and too long.

As in El Paso, leaders in Pueblo's Compact launched their own standard-setting process and are participating in the standards-based professional development initiative funded by the Fund for the Improvement of Education. The context is different, however, because the State of Colorado encouraged local standard-setting beginning in 1994–1995. The Colorado Department of Education created a set of model standards, then challenged local districts to develop their own—as high or higher. These are then reviewed by a state panel. Pueblo's standards were completed in 1996.

One of the most interesting aspects of the work in Pueblo is the Compact's effort to analyze and report student outcomes for K–12 and higher education. From the beginning, leaders in the Compact made a commitment to release initial data and then report regularly to their community on progress. But when they saw the results of the Compact staff's data collection and analysis, several grew worried about its impact on public trust. Particularly worrisome were data showing that about one-half of the students who began ninth grade did not finish high school, yet, in accordance with national practice, the school district had been reporting an official annual drop-out rate considerably lower than that.

Compact Coordinator LeAnn Withnell prepared the ground for initial release by taking school-by-school data to local middle and senior high schools and sharing it with the principal and faculty. Her purpose was to begin conversations about how to improve the performance data, which showed not only high attrition but also low numbers of students enrolled and succeeding in college preparatory classes. Most of the teachers had never seen the data, much less been involved in thinking about how to improve it.

The leaders in the Compact prepared a public report and organized a forum where they could share the data publicly. Just as leaders in other cities have learned when they take the initiative and release their own data instead of waiting for an expose, the leaders in Pueblo found the reporting process invaluable in galvanizing their community around the problem of underachievement—a problem that, according to a local business leader, "we all own."

Now, everyone in Pueblo is working to prepare all Pueblo students to meet the standards. Indeed, the school district is the first in the nation to implement standards-based graduation, beginning in 2001.

Los Angeles/Northridge

The San Fernando Valley or "Northridge" area of Los Angeles is the seat of a recently launched a "Pre-K to 16" reform initiative. Even though her institution was still recovering from the earthquake that closed it in 1993, Blenda Wilson, president of California State University Northridge (CSUN), was determined both to press for improvement at CSUN and to reach out to nearby schools. She found an enthusiastic partner in Yvonne Davis, administrative head of the Grant/Van Nuys cluster of the Los Angeles Unified School District, which serves approximately 26,000 students, a majority of whom are Latino.

With able assistance from organizational change experts at the Los Angeles–based Achievement Council, an independent organization working to improve achievement and college-going rates among Latino, African American, and poor students, the two education leaders launched their own K–16 reform effort. Los Angeles Valley College, a two-year institution, is also actively involved.

Unlike some cities embarking on K–16 reform efforts, the leaders in the Northridge/LA K–16 Council are very clear that their plans involve equal change efforts at both levels. Indeed, rather than fashioning institutes to engage school teams in analyzing their data and planning for improvement, the LA institutes have involved teams of administrators and faculty at both levels.

Experiences like these can be most profound for higher educa- tion faculty. Unlike their counterparts in K–12, most of whom have years of experience with public reports of test scores and drop-out rates, most college faculty members have no idea what student per- sistence rates are in their institution as a whole, much less in their departments. Further, they have never analyzed data on students majoring in their field to identify patterns among students in par- ticular groups, identify problem courses, and decide how to respond. The LA K–16 initiative is pioneering new strategies to begin such conversations and to link them with parallel conversa- tions in K–12.

The CSUN portion of the change strategy is guided by the provost and a committee of faculty and deans called the Commit- tee on Change. Composed of staff members with records of inter- est and success in improving learning, especially among minority students, the Committee on Change is working to develop strate- gies to involve faculty members across the institution. To give them time for their work, the president and provost have reduced course loads for several committee leaders.

CSUN is also one of three universities, along with Temple University and the University of Texas at El Paso, where higher education leaders have committed themselves to devising ways to systematically reward faculty members who participate in such efforts. They are currently working together in a project funded by the Fund for the Improvement of Postsecondary Education to develop ways of recording and evaluating faculty contribution to K–16 reform, as well as methods for rewarding such work.

Key Tasks for Higher Education in Systemic Reform

As leaders in K–12 began the shift toward a systemic approach to reform, the question for leaders in higher education was whether they, too, could or should make the shift. Although higher education might do this in a variety of ways, there are some tasks in systemic reform for which college and university involvement seems to be more important than in others.

Task 1: Communicating the Need for Reform

State and local leaders in K–12 education have been working hard to build community understanding of the critical importance of reform—in all schools. So, too, have governors and business leaders, but leaders in higher education have been remarkably silent. Only rarely does a college president or senior member of the faculty sit shoulder to shoulder with the local superintendent of schools in explaining changes in the workplace and in society more generally—and what those changes require by way of reform. Leaders in higher education need to join in the effort to build understanding of the need for school reform.

Task 2: Helping to Develop Standards for What Students Should Know and Be Able to Do

Over the past two years, voluntary national standards have been released describing what students should know and be able to do in virtually all of the core disciplines. States and, in some cases, local communities are now responsible, as a part of their obligations under Goals: 2000 and the Elementary and Secondary Education Acts, for developing their own standards.

It is essential that postsecondary institutions, their faculty members and leaders, join in this process and become active in the establishment of statewide K–12 standards. Even more important, college and university faculty members should join with their counterparts in K–12 in a local process of reviewing the national and state standards documents, examining samples of student work to see whether it meets the standards, and deciding what can be done in the classroom to help students reach the standards. This local process is critically important if local educators are to see standards as "theirs" and worthy of their best effort.

Task 3: Reinforcing New Standards with Revised College Admissions and Placement Practices

Though the task is not an easy one, higher education must get about the business of expressing its standards—for admission and placement, if not also for graduation—in nomenclature that is consistent with that in K–12 and that will send consistent signals to students, teachers, and parents. Instead of complaining about how much harder it is to "rank" portfolios compared to grade-point averages and SAT scores, higher educators should join together with colleagues in K-12 to develop high-quality standards and performance assessments.

Task 4: Teacher Professional Development

Since the publication of A *Nation at Risk*, the nation's colleges and universities have created a host of programs that help teachers to deepen their knowledge and improve instruction. Colleges also offer advanced academic coursework that has a pronounced effect on enabling teachers to improve student achievement. Yet these vehicles serve too few of the teachers who need them. Moreover, they are often neither intense enough nor sufficiently connected to the school setting to result in enduring changes in classroom practice.

Higher education needs to cooperate with K–12—with schools, school districts, teacher associations, and the like—to build an infrastructure capable of aiding in the professional development of all of our teachers. This infrastructure must include faculty from the arts and sciences, not just education professors. Like other professionals, teachers need regular means to stay abreast of developments in their fields and ongoing support for improving their practice.

Task 5: Pre-Service Preparation

The preparation of new teachers should be aligned as closely as possible with the imperatives of systemic K–12 education reform. This is particularly important in relation to new standards for student achievement in the disciplines, for which the content knowledge of teachers will be especially critical. On this point, college and university leaders have an opportunity to encourage new ways of thinking about the involvement of arts and sciences faculty in teacher education. What if, for example, academic faculty had to certify that all students preparing for teaching careers in middle and high school had sufficient grasp of the domains covered in the standards for that discipline? Would this help to bridge the schism between faculties in education and the arts and sciences? Would it result in better teachers? Would it draw greater attention to the quality of teaching within the arts and science courses themselves?

What about recruitment of the best and brightest for K–12 teaching careers? The success of standards-based reform will depend not just on preparation but on the recruitment and retention of the best students in our postsecondary institutions, particularly those from racial and ethnic groups, which form the majority of schoolchildren in many urban and other districts. In this regard what can higher education learn from Teach for America? How can community service activities be connected to the identification of future teachers?

Task 6: Reframing Higher Education's Research Agenda and Sharing Results

In recent years, researchers in colleges and universities have made great advances in understanding the human brain and how people learn. Further, we know considerably more now than we did before about the interconnections among health, psychological well-being, and learning. Yet academic researchers have not invested much energy in communicating their findings in ways that are useful to pre-collegiate educators. Leaders in higher education need to create vehicles for sharing advances in knowledge in these and other fields with child-serving professionals.

We also need to create vehicles that allow these professionals to help shape higher education research priorities. Many teachers and educational administrators believe that college professors conduct research on everything but what is important to them. We need to find ways to better connect teachers' needs with scholars' research capacities. One area of special need is research on the impact of the systemic reform strategies now being implemented at the K–12 level.

Task 7: Higher Education Reform

Though data on student outcomes in higher education are not nearly as plentiful as in K–12, available data suggest that outcomes in colleges and universities are far from satisfactory. Drop-out rates in higher education as a whole are higher than those of the worst urban high schools, and those among minority students are especially high. Further, recent analyses of various data sources, including NAEP's 1992 study of adult literacy, suggest that many college graduates do not have the knowledge and skills that most people normally associate with a college degree (Educational Testing Service, 1995).

There are, in other words, reasons beyond the need to help out with K–12 reform that ought to impel a similar effort in higher education. Early evidence from some of the Compact and K–16 cities indicates that many of the same strategies—establishing clearer learning goals, developing assessment strategies to measure progress toward the goals, devolving authority, and so on—are equally appropriate in higher education.

Encouraging K–16 Reform

Interest in K–16 approaches to reform is growing each year, especially in urban areas where school districts and colleges share the same student population and budget and political pressures are intense. But the need for such approaches vastly exceeds the response. What might policymakers—national or state—do to encourage more higher education involvement in K–16 reform?

- *Obtain better information about student outcomes in grades 13–16.* Regular public reports from NAEP, Educational Testing Service, and various international sources about knowledge and skills among American elementary and secondary students have helped education professionals and the public at large to evaluate the performance of the K–12 system and have fueled the current reform effort. The absence of similar information at the postsecondary level reinforces the sense of complacency among postsecondary educators and the public about the quality of our higher education system. Concerned policymakers need to authorize and finance periodic examinations of core knowledge and skills among college graduates, including comparisons with students abroad.

- *Require accountability for student outcomes.* In the past several years, policymakers have insisted on greater accountability from both the K–12 and higher education systems. In K–12, the emphasis has shifted from monitoring processes to improving student outcomes. Oddly, in higher education, the new emphasis is on productivity, measured in process terms like *faculty course loads*. If energy and attention is usually directed to what is measured, the results are predictable. Policymakers who wish to improve student learning outcomes in higher education ought to insist on accountability structures that identify and reward improved outcomes, especially among underachieving groups.

- *Review faculty reward systems.* Recent polls of higher education faculty members suggest that large numbers of the faculty now believe—as have policymakers and the public for some time—that the reward structure is too lopsided in favoring research at the expense of teaching and service. Many institutions are now immersed in reexamining their reward structures. Interested policymakers should support and encourage these efforts and demand concrete evidence of change.

- *Support development of standards for college admissions and placement.* Policymakers should insist that higher education faculty play a significant role in developing standards for K–12 students, and that higher education's admissions and placement systems reflect the new standards. In addition, support should be provided for efforts by postsecondary faculties to clarify their goals for their own students.

• *Encourage innovative alternatives to remedial coursework.* Judging from the current frenzy in the media and in policy circles, one would think that remedial education is a new phenomenon in American colleges and universities. Nonetheless, institutions of higher education—including highly selective universities—have held significant numbers of their students for "remedial" courses for more than one hundred years. Rather than fueling the rather simplistic finger-pointing that is going on across the wall that separates our K–12 and higher education systems, concerned policymakers should encourage and support efforts—like the CUNY/NY City Schools College Preparatory Initiative, for example—that bring educational issues to the fore and that promote cooperative solutions. The foundation laid in this multi-year initiative resulted in CUNY's best-prepared freshman class in years: 1995 freshmen were held for fewer remedial courses than at any time during the past decade.

• *Finance K–16 reform.* Our experience suggests that K–16 style reform efforts proceed faster and more smoothly if they receive some direct financial support. Indeed, many promising efforts have floundered because their leaders cannot find the small amount of support necessary to move them along, including support for staff to coordinate the effort and funds for planning meetings, retreats, and data analysis. Acknowledging this need, the university system of Georgia has recently just launched an initiative to provide seed money for fifteen local "P–16" reform efforts. Policymakers should support similar efforts elsewhere.

By making these and other policy changes, policymakers can create an environment that encourages cooperation rather than competition and finger-pointing among leaders in K–12 and higher education. In the end, however, the action must come from the leaders themselves. The work of bringing about systemic change—especially in multiple institutions simultaneously—is very, very difficult. It demands incredible amounts of time and energy. Only leaders who are truly committed to the notion that their institutions can and must significantly improve student learning and who are relentless in their focus will weather the storms that deep change efforts inevitably incur. Even the most committed educators will need to build and continuously nurture linkages with other influential players—political, business, and community—if they are to maintain the support they need to see positive results from their efforts.

References

Brubacher, J. S., and Rudy, W. *Higher Education in Transition: An American History, 1636–1956.* New York: HarperCollins, 1958.

Educational Testing Service. *Learning by Degree.* Princeton, N.J.: Educational Testing Service, 1995.

National Commission on Excellence in Education. *A Nation at Risk.* Washington, D.C.: National Commission on Excellence in Education, 1983.

Wilbur, F., and Lambert, L. *Linking America's Schools and Colleges.* (2nd ed.) Bolton, Mass.: Anker, 1995.

Chapter Five

The Challenge Teacher Education Presents for Higher Education

Frank B. Murray

The primary and overriding goal of the modern school reform movement, which drives all other goals of school reform, is to have *all* the school's pupils *understand*, not just learn, their lessons (Gardner, 1991). Of course, students have always been expected to learn their lessons and pass school tests on what they have learned, but contemporary school reformers now hold a higher standard for schooling—that the students understand and *do the subject*, so to speak. Understanding, clearly a more ambitious undertaking for the student and the teacher, represents a qualitative change in the school's agenda and the mental life of the student. Understanding what is learned entails a connection to a framework or explanatory system. The construction of this framework requires a different kind of relationship between the student and teacher and a different kind of work from each.

Consider the following school problem: If there is a 15 percent discount and a 15 percent tax on merchandise, does it matter in which order the salesperson does each operation, namely, compute the discount first, tax second, or vice versa? It would be one thing to have simply learned, even memorized the answer, that the order makes no difference. It is quite another to understand, not just that the order makes no difference, but that it *has* to make no difference and that, regardless of any particular price and percentage, the order would always have to make no difference. The fact that the order makes no difference is understood when it is placed in, or derived from, a system of algebraic expressions that makes the outcome a matter of necessity.

This emphasis on understanding is the goal of today's school reformers, and this new goal inevitably places a significant burden on the teacher education curriculum as it is found in American higher education.

Some Features of the New Schools That Affect Higher Education

Modern teacher education degree programs are asked to take teachers beyond their usual enthusiastic assent to the many laudable reform slogans, such as "all kids can learn" or "less is more." The public asks only one thing of higher education—that it be the source of clear, authoritative, and penetrating thought on important matters. To move beyond the reform slogans, higher education must promote the new teacher's deep understanding of the slogans and the following core features of modern schooling and teaching:

• *Standards and scoring rubrics*. Teachers need a way to formulate standards for their student's intellectual and academic accomplishments, especially the degree to which each pupil has understood each subject studied in the school. The standards, implicitly applied in the teacher's traditional and daily evaluation of each pupil's work, are now asked to be made explicit. This means that the criteria by which all can know whether a student's work meets the standard, is well below it, or is well above it must be formulated and made public. The scoring rubric, by which the student's accomplishments and progress are noted, is at the heart of the matter and is inherently dependent upon the teacher's theory (naive or sophisticated) of at least two domains: a theory of children's and adolescent's cognitive development and understanding, and a theory of the complexity and sophistication of the subject matter itself. Both domains are represented in the well-worn example of a child who had pluralized *mouse* as *mice* and suddenly pluralizes it as *mouses*. A naive teacher might score the event as an unfortunate regression that requires remediation, whereas a professional teacher will see the *error* as temporary and actually as a sign of cognitive advancement in which the pupil is exhibiting a newly developed appreciation of a linguistic rule that is merely overgeneralized in this instance.

Upon what theory, to take another example, is the teacher to score the pupil who arrives at the correct answer to a multiplication problem through serial addition lower or higher than the pupil who arrives at an incorrect answer through multiplication?

The new teacher will need to have a solid understanding of the discipline so that she can tell which of the pupil's subject matter conceptions are more sophisticated, elegant, powerful than other conceptions. How will the teacher determine which subject matter concepts are more advanced (above the standard, etc.): those that came later historically, those espoused by older students, those that have greater *meaning* for the student, or those that conform to the higher education curriculum? The answer is complicated and a case can be made for each of the alternatives mentioned above.

To see how complicated, consider another school problem: How many games of checkers need to be played in a classroom of twenty-four students to find the champion checker player of the class? Consider further the following responses that students might give in response to this question:

This is too complicated to work out in one's head, I would have no idea.

Somewhere between 20 and 50 games and certainly fewer than 100 would be needed to find the champion, I think.

You really can't tell ahead of time because it would depend upon who won and lost early. It could go in different directions, some would require more games and some would need fewer games. It all depends.

Well, in the first round, 12 games are needed and you get 12 winners and 12 losers. Then, 6 games are needed for the 12 winners, and then 3 games for the 6 winners in the second round. Then, 2 more games for the 3 winners in the third round to get 1 champion. So, you need 12+6+3+2 games, which adds up to 23 games.

(A second student might go through all these steps, but add 12+6+3+2 differently for a different total, say 21 games.)

If there are 24 students in the class, 23 have to lose a game, so 23 games would be needed.

On what body of knowledge would the teacher draw to determine which of the above responses was below standard, met the standard, or exceeded the standard for this kind of school problem? Where in the university's teacher education program would the teacher receive guidance in how to score these responses and see which are on the right track and merit encouragement of the pupil and which should be shifted to other directions?

Whatever the answer, the study of subject matter in the teacher education program needs to yield guidance for these kinds of questions—questions that the teacher cannot avoid in the evaluation of student subject matter performance and questions for which higher education is expected to provide answers.

In addition to the deep study of subject matter, the teacher education program needs to supply guidance in the second domain cited above, namely the study of the child's mind and its development. If the school, for example, had as part of the elementary science standard the requirement that the primary school pupil know how to change the weight of a clay ball, the teacher would need to understand more than the physics of the situation.

The literature in child development converges on the following picture of the child's thinking about the weight of objects. It can be shown that first-graders and many second-graders believe the weight of the clay ball can be changed in many ways. The ball's weight would change if the ball were made larger or smaller, if it were flattened, if its surface was roughened or smoothed, if it were chilled or warmed (that is, made hard or soft), if it were broken into pieces, if it could be simply called *larger* or *smaller* than it was before (it could be called *larger* if it were next to a small ball and it could be called *smaller* if it were next to a large ball, for example), but it would not change if it were simply moved from one end of the table to another or moved from the basement to the attic (Murray and Johnson, 1970, 1975).

The young child's view of weight is based upon a consistent child-logic that conceals many misconceptions about weight. These misconceptions, obviously, have implications for pedagogy and the teacher's evaluation of the pupil's work, especially whether the pupil is below, at, or above a standard set by the school or the state (Murray, 1982; Murray and Markessini, 1982).

There is a similar developmental progression, incidentally, for the child's understanding of the beam balance in which the young child's understanding of *weighing* is controlled solely by the effects of adding or subtracting weight from a beam balance pan without regard to the influence of any other factor (Siegler, 1981). Later, the distance of the balance pan from the fulcrum is gradually factored into the child's scheme for the operation of the balance, and after several more developmental steps we see the product moment law in place in the adolescent's thinking.

• *Important ideas.* Because students require more time to understand material than to learn material, the school curriculum will be restricted inevitably to matters that are thought to be indispensable to a life of the mind and the life of the nation. Again, upon what theory is this reduction in the content of the curriculum to take place? How is the teacher to figure out which ideas, of all the concepts in the current curriculum, are worth a significant investment in instructional time and which should be slighted? Should the elementary school curriculum, for example, dispense with fractions and focus on decimals or the other way around? This question hopes for a *less is more* answer, in the sense that while the student will be exposed to less information, she will understand what is taught so that she ends up having more. The answer is intellectually demanding, calling, as it does, for educators to justify that some topics are more important than others. The contemporary university curriculum with its massive number of options and electives rarely takes a stand on the issue of what knowledge is of most worth and, on the face of it, would not seem to be a good source of assistance with this problem.

• *Dialectical instruction.* Understanding cannot be produced by the teacher's art alone, by didactic telling, or by showing and coaching, as valuable as each are on occasion. Although it is important on many occasions for the pupil to learn and remember what the teacher said or to imitate what the teacher did, understanding requires more. Understanding, in contrast, is dependent upon dialectic—upon the pupil's active thought, investigation, and experimentation, guided, when necessary, by the teacher's skillful questioning and conversation.

The pupil, for example, cannot be given, simply told, or shown the idea of necessity by her teacher. Although she can be told and shown that the whole is greater than any of its parts and learn the truth of that relationship that way, she cannot understand that the whole *must* be greater by the assertion or demonstration that it is so. Rather the pupil must invent the idea of necessity and other pivotal concepts (like time, justice, and cause). Unlike *solutions* that are learned, the dialectically acquired outcomes, like knowing which truths are true of necessity, are personal and extraordinarily resistant to forgetting. With the exception of the doctoral seminar, university instruction rarely provides much opportunity for dialectical styles of pedagogy.

• *Modern views of intelligence.* Pupils will not understand their lessons about pivotal concepts if the teacher's role is merely to deliver information, however important information is in high-level thinking. While dialectic requires the pupil to do something overtly—to speak, respond, and question—there are other features of teaching for understanding that require the pupil to be active because nothing will be understood if the pupil is not active.

Regardless of how well the school is managed, the teacher does not in fact have the power to transfer knowledge to the pupil, and this means that the student's intellectual cooperation is a precondition of his inventing what he comes to know and understand. The teacher must begin the lessons with what the student brings to the lesson; they must negotiate what is important and privileged and to what aspects of the student's prior understanding the lesson will be linked and assimilated.

Because the range of things to be known and understood exceeds the cognitive capacities of our minds, knowing must be distributed across technological devices, books, lists, and, increasingly, other people with whom we must cooperate and interact. The amount of mental space available for active processing is severely limited (perhaps to as few as seven simultaneous or unrelated events), and consequently complex thought is critically dependent upon other devices for assisting the mind in its handling the other factors imbedded in complex problems.

In particular, the use of computer technology in the classroom not only shifts instruction from the teacher to the student but shifts the student's activity from learning to understanding (Sheingold, 1991). Interactive computer programs irrevocably change the predetermined sequential nature of the school curriculum, the authority for knowledge, and generally force instruction into a modern format (for example, Scardamalia and Bereiter, 1991).

In the last several years the cognitive science literature consistently demonstrates that understanding is also dependent upon, and critically shaped by, its context or its place—by the situation in which it takes place. It proves very difficult to document aspects of thought that transcend particular circumstances and generalize as widely as traditional school pedagogy and curricula assume.

Several lines of theory also suggest that what we understand is best seen as an invention or construction, provisionally and personally erected to permit sense to be made of a particular set of physical, social, and historical factors. These mental constructions also seem to be qualitatively different from each other over time as they are based upon different mechanisms and logic. It is not simply that the older pupil has more information than the younger one, which of course she does, but rather that the older pupil reasons in a new and novel manner that is not available to the younger pupil or sometimes to the adult teacher. The pupil's understanding, in other words, cannot be reduced or decomposed into the intellectual possessions of her younger self. Her new understanding emerges from her prior understanding the way *wetness* emerges from the combination of two gasses, oxygen and hydrogen, or the way a butterfly emerges from the caterpillar. The later constructions cannot be predicted from any features of the child's prior understanding, just as wetness could not be predicted from any feature of a gas, or a gas from any feature of a liquid (Murray, 1992).

Finally, cognition and intellectual functioning are increasingly seen as integrated with the other features of the mind. The systematic and ancient links between knowing, emotion, and motivation must be respected in pedagogy, as knowing is surely in the primary service of pervasive and powerful noncognitive factors.

When universities rely, as they typically do, on large lecture formats for the majority of the degree program course of study, it is clear that most of these features of modern cognitive psychology are ignored or minimized. Thus, the transfer of modern instructional practice from higher to lower education is not assured.

Higher Education's Role and Obligation in School Reform

For other reasons that will be clearer later, there is some doubt about what contemporary higher education has to offer the new teacher in this ambitious program of school reform. There are four basic and straightforward questions that need to be collectively answered by the higher education community before it is clear that the liberal arts or teacher education curricula can assist the new teacher in the challenge of teaching for understanding. One higher education reform group, the Project 30 Alliance, has organized its work as a collaborative of liberal arts and education faculty members around the following four issues (Murray and Fallon, 1989):

• *Question 1: Subject matter understanding.* How should teachers acquire knowledge of the discipline(s) they are licensed to teach? The traditional college major would seem to be the right answer to this question, but it is not the complete answer, as it can be shown to be insufficient, and sometimes misleading, preparation for the teacher (McDiarmid, 1990).

- *Question 2: General and liberal knowledge.* How do teacher education graduates become well-informed persons? Beyond being well-informed, however, how do prospective teachers come to have the habits of mind that have always been claimed for a liberal education? These habits are essential if teachers are to become more than technicians.

- *Question 3: Pedagogical content knowledge.* How do teacher education students learn to convert their knowledge of the subject matter into lessons for a wide range of pupils? This is the weakest link in teacher education programs and the area that requires the most intense cooperation between faculties in education and in the arts and sciences.

- *Question 4: Multicultural, international, and other human perspectives.* For all persons, but especially for prospective teachers, the college curriculum must be accurate with respect to the best scholarship on matters of race, gender, ethnic, and cultural perspective. Making the curriculum accurate in this way is difficult in view of the fact that scholarship is often incomplete and merely suggestive and most higher education faculty were educated in a period when there was very little sensitivity to, or awareness of, alternative perspectives in each curricular domain. How will teachers, moreover, acquire the dispositions to act on their new knowledge in the sensitive and accepting manner that leads to high levels of achievement for all their pupils?

Question 1: How Should Teachers Learn the Subjects They Will Teach?

By and large, the traditional academic major, as it is geared toward graduate study or entry level employment, does not lead students to the kind of basic understanding necessary to be an effective teacher (Kennedy, 1991). Apart from the purposes of the major, there are problems with the scope of its contents for some teaching assignments like elementary school teaching. The prospective elementary teacher, for example, needs to be well-grounded in mathematics, literature, writing, history, geography, the natural and social sciences, the fine arts, language, and much more. Similar problems are found at the secondary level in social studies or general science teaching, which are informed by several distinct university subjects or majors, each of which is a full university course of study in its own right (see Murray, 1991a, for an extended treatment of appropriate liberal arts majors for elementary school teachers).

We do know that reasonably well-educated college and university graduates find themselves in difficulty in their attempts to answer coherently, and with integrity, the questions that young children are likely to put to them (Ball, 1991). Ball (1990) reported, for example, that mathematics majors were no more successful than non-majors were in thinking of real-world events that corresponded, for example, to the arithmetical problem, "divide the fraction 1¾ by the fraction ½." Besides making the mistake of providing examples of dividing by 2 instead of ½, the majors in mathematics did not have the kind of mathematical understanding that would support the teaching of this and other elementary mathematical topics.

A new kind of academic major for teachers must be invented and established in higher education. This major, a mixture of subject matter and child development, would provide the teacher with a way of determining whether the pupil's performance is *developmentally* or *cognitively* above, at, or below an academic standard. It entails a combination of the study of the developmental origins and maturation of our basic notions of the universe and ourselves.

In this approach the teacher education student learns the relevant developmental constraints upon the pupil's acquisition of the curriculum and also learns, as an unavoidable part of the discussion, the nature of the subject matter itself. The story of how the young child develops the notion of number, for example, is valuable in its own right, but it also reveals salient portions of number theory, the arithmetical algorithms, and other aspects of mathematics. Similarly, the account of the child's moral development reveals the principal issues in moral philosophy and political theory, for example.

All concepts and relations in the curriculum can be profitably approached from this perspective. The approach also has face validity in teacher education because it contains the kinds of information that prospective teachers accept as clearly relevant for their future work, particularly the evaluation of whether the pupil's understanding meets a content standard.

The prospective teacher's study of children's subject matter thinking, however, is more than a device by which students in teacher education might learn their academic disciplines. It goes to the core of the kind of knowledge the teacher needs, namely generative ways of organizing information and knowledge. It entails the search for structures, alternate ways of representing the subject matter, analogies and metaphors, that could take *each* pupil well beyond what can be held together temporally and spatially through rote memorization.

Question 2: What Are the Uses of a Liberal Arts Education in Teacher Education?

Almost every educational reform report has made the unchallenged claim that teachers need to be well schooled in the liberal arts. Sometimes the claim for the liberal arts has been made on the grounds that teachers ought to be well-informed persons, and well-informed persons are those, and only those, who have been schooled in the liberal arts. Even here, there is confusion because being well-informed is not the same thing as being liberally educated. General and liberal education are about different things— the one being about having good and dependable information and the other about knowing what the point of something is and what is worth doing (Blits, 1985).

Question 2 is about knowledge and information that the teacher does not teach directly and may not ever teach, yet it is about knowledge that is presumed to influence teaching, and other human endeavors, in several important ways.

The liberal arts are those subjects that are worth knowing for their own sake; they are ends in themselves, activities that make human life complete. They are studies that are appropriate for the free person, the person who is free of utilitarian concerns, free from the need of labor; in other words, they are studies that are appropriate for leisure.

They are studies that set the student free in another sense as well—free from the bondage of convention, unanalyzed custom and opinion, free of the tyranny of dogma and assertion, and free to search out and construct truth. They show the student how, by the power of human reason, to search for and construct truth—truths not heretofore known and truths that are inevitably provisional because all the thinkers have not, and cannot have, completed their work.

While the actual content of the liberal course of study may be somewhat arbitrary, its outcome is not—it must take even the successful teacher beyond technique and algorithms.

Question 3: How Are Academic Disciplines Transformed into School Lessons?

All teachers know that the subject matter they teach is different from the subject matter they learned from their own teachers. The teacher inevitably transforms the subject matter into something else—a teachable subject that has its own structure and logic and is something that will help the student make sense of the subject matter.

The knowledge that supports this conversion of the storehouse of knowledge into the school curriculum, into something that has meaning for the pupil, is sometimes called *pedagogical content knowledge* (Shulman, 1986, 1987). As an example, the young elementary school child will be taught one of the algorithms for subtraction.

There are several options for taking 67 from 95, for example. The two numbers in the problem can be regrouped and represented as (60 + 7) taken from (80 + 15), by a strategy known as *decomposition*, or the numbers in the problem may be represented as (70 + 7) taken from (90 + 15), by a strategy known as *equal additions*. Or, more elaborate and equally correct algorithms can be taught in which the correct answer, 28, is had by making different combinations of calculations that are also sound and academically sensible. (The subtrahend, 67, for example, can be taken from 100 and the difference, 33, added to the minuend, 95, to give 128. When the 1 in 128 is discarded, the correct answer, 28, remains.) On what basis should the teacher choose an algorithm for the lesson inasmuch as mathematically there is no basis for selecting one algorithm over another, except perhaps on elegance or parsimony? Kamii (1989) found, for example, that young children invent yet other strategies that are a more natural outgrowth of the young child's understanding of number than are the usual school taught algorithms of decomposition or equal additions.

Consider teaching the division of "1¾ by ½" mentioned above, and going beyond the traditional algorithm, *invert and multiply*. If the teacher were asked for some real-world examples of this arithmetical operation, what would the teacher have had to study to develop a repertoire of different representations of the arithmetical expression, 1¾ ÷ ½? (For example, "How many 50 cent tickets be bought with $1.75?" or "How many half-yard ruffles can be sewn from 1¾ yards of ruffles?" or "How many halves of pizza can be served from 1¾ pizzas?" or "How many dips of a ½ quart container of oil are needed to exactly fill an engine that holds only 1¾ quarts?" and so on.) Whatever the discipline might be called, it is a new kind of knowledge that is dependent upon a knowledge of fractions, but is not directly derivable from it, and as such it is qualitatively different from it. Moreover, this new kind of knowledge must also consider the fact that some of these of representations, specifically the pizza pie representation, may actually interfere with the pupil's understanding of fractions.

This knowledge—the knowledge of what is a telling example, a good analogy, algorithm or heuristic, a provocative question, a compelling theme—is a proper, and unfortunately a neglected, object of study by educators and could yield a deep and generative understanding of the disciplines. To have multiple ways of representing a subject matter, to have more than one example or metaphor, to have more than one mode of explanation requires a high-order and demanding form of subject matter understanding. Where in the university is the new teacher to find pedagogical content knowledge as an object of undergraduate inquiry?

Educational critics often say that, owing to the low quality of teaching, school pupils and university students are driven to memorize by rote large portions of the curriculum. The point of education, as a result, seems to be little more than to return this memorized and undigested material to the teacher on an examination. However, the human mind cannot memorize very much material by rote, as we have noted. Even the marginal pupil who confronts the massive amounts of material in the school and university curriculum finds a way to impose some structure, some organizational scheme, on the material. The question is never whether or not there was some structure, theory, scheme, etc., but only whether the structure was good or poor—above, below, or at standard. Whatever the teacher actually did in the lesson, the pupils will find some way to make sense of it, to code it, to assimilate it into what they already know, often with an outcome the teacher may never have intended.

In the end, the discussion of pedagogical content knowledge becomes a discussion of the appropriate ways of organizing information and knowledge. At the lowest pedagogical content knowledge level, there are mnemonic structures that can carry the student past the half-dozen memorized items, but these structures accomplish very little other than improving retention and defending the memorized items against the rapid forgetting that is the hallmark of most learned material learned by rote. The mnemonic device, *roygbiv* can provide the student with the order of the spectral colors (namely, red, orange, yellow, etc.). Like all mnemonic devices, however, it fails to provide understanding —it gives no clue about how or why the spectral order takes place, or why the order of colors is reversed in the second rainbow of a double set, and so on. Knowing the order of the spectral colors can be very helpful and may be essential information for the solution to many higher-order problems, for example, but understanding requires more than this. Pedagogical content knowledge is fundamentally about those structures that confer some appropriate level of understanding, and it is ultimately about those structures that actually advance our understanding.

The invention of these pedagogical representations can be quite difficult and can be contributions to the field when they occur at the cutting edge. The inventions of the periodic table and the double helix, for example, are inherently pedagogical in that they permitted researchers at the cutting edge to comprehend, much as the novice student does, an otherwise bewildering array of data. They enabled researchers to teach each other. Of course, at this level these *pedagogical* structures advance an entire field.

When the teacher invents a structure that organizes and gives meaning to a school subject, he or she may be doing *exactly* what the scholar or researcher does when the scholar provides a novel or generative structure for his or her peers about some problem in their field. Thus, the study of pedagogical content knowledge can be a study on the cutting edge of a field, insofar as new modes of representing the subject matter and new ways of making it interesting and meaningful are formulated.

Question 4: How Can the Teacher Education Curriculum Be Made More Accurate?

Tomorrow's teachers will face classrooms of pupils that will be markedly more diverse and varied than the pupils in today's classrooms. Tomorrow's teachers and tomorrow's pupils are becoming very different from each other.

The issue of cultural diversity is not a peripheral matter or merely a desirable add-on to the teacher education curriculum. The issue is at the heart of school reform because the honesty and accuracy of the curriculum is at stake. The charge that higher education is parochial and insensitive to international and global matters as well as to matters of significance to the nation's many minority groups is fundamentally a charge that the curriculum is wrong, the very thing it cannot be! To give only one example, the discipline of psychology turns out to be very different from what is presented in the standard introductory textbook when it is qualified by the contributions of African American psychologists (Guthrie, 1976).

The point is that the study of minority issues or the study of global or international issues will fail, as they have in the past, if they are not anchored, passionately and with conviction, in the core values of the academy. Undoubtedly short-term gains can be had from attempts to secure a place for these matters in federal law and regulation, in arguments about compensation for past injustice, in assertions about fairness and decency, in appeals to the specter of failure in the international markets, or in the realization that minorities can exert political power over the allocation of public dollars. They will fail ultimately to win a place for cultural diversity in higher education, however, because each effort can be deflected so easily by its politically incorrect critics when it is based only on these short-term considerations and arguments.

At each stage of cognitive development, an individual's cognitive growth is enhanced by the confrontation of divergent views, by the clash of paradigms, perspectives, and theories. The history of the great universities is largely the story of an ever widening inclusion, however slow, of different groups and views—inclusion based in part on inclusion as a value in its own right. More importantly, the core values of the academy are enhanced by the inclusion of more groups—both among the students and the faculty—in the quest for a more coherent account of things. Intellectual evolution, like biological evolution, is dependent upon a base of variability, a base of multiple perspectives and interests, a base that contains many different kinds of candidates for success.

The prospective teacher, however, needs more than a firm grasp of a new subject matter that is shaped by important modern and postmodern scholarship and by the political tension between Western traditionalists, multiculturalists, and Afrocentrists (Banks, 1993). Though knowledge that has the potential to transform the prospective teacher's views is vital, it is inevitably limited, and the diversity in tomorrow's classroom can be expected to exceed the diversity in today's teacher education curriculum. There can never be, for all practical purposes, a close match between the deep knowledge of various cultures and language groups, no matter how sophisticated the university, and the actual variation a teacher can expect to find in any classroom of a large urban school system, several of which have speakers from more than 100 different language groups. Consequently, the teacher cannot be expected actually to know that, for example, an Eskimo child might resist summarizing a story because his culture has a prohibition of speaking for another, or that some Native American students might subvert the school's policy on cheating because they adhere to cultural policy of cooperation among peers, or that the Hispanic child's avoidance of a disciplinarian's eyes signifies something different from what it typically indicates for some other groups.

Rather, the prospective teacher has little option but to acquire attitudes and skills similar to those of the teacher of English as a Second Language (ESL). These teachers teach English to classrooms of students, none of whom know English and all of whom speak a language the ESL teacher does not, or need not, speak. The ESL teacher's attitude, disposition, and skill, admittedly focussed on language teaching, carry equal force in the teaching of other subject matters to students with diverse backgrounds.

The Case for University-Based Teacher Education

Despite the documented shortcomings in the liberal arts curriculum, there is a resurgence of the popular view that the nation's need for new teachers can be provided by well-meaning liberal arts graduates who are willing to sacrifice temporarily the career benefits of their degrees to work in the schools. This view takes comfort in the analogy that the needs of higher education have been traditionally met by those who are trained to research their subject and who are willing to accept positions as college instructors. This argument against professional teacher education relies heavily on the fact that teaching is a naturally occurring human behavior that precedes formal schooling and formal teacher education by several centuries. Teaching is a natural act and a longstanding feature of the ancient repertoire of human behaviors. The question is whether university- and college-based teacher education offers anything that can take novices much beyond the natural teaching skills all persons have.

J. M. Stephens (1967) catalogued the features of naturally occurring teaching in his theory of spontaneous schooling. His argument was that schooling, a feature of all anthropological groups, was dependent on a set of natural human tendencies that some persons had to greater degrees than others. Those that had these tendencies in generous proportions would be teachers, whether they intended to be or not. Teaching and learning would take place naturally and not with any particular motive to benefit the pupil. They would occur merely because the tendencies, which served the teacher's own needs, led incidentally, but inevitably, to learning in those persons in the teacher's company. Teaching, in other words, was spontaneous and non-deliberate and occurred whenever a person with these tendencies was with any other person.

The theory of spontaneous schooling was put forth to account for two pervasive findings—the universality of schooling and the fact that most educational research overwhelmingly finds insignificant differences between educational treatments. It accounts for universality by arguing that wherever there are people, there are these spontaneous tendencies, and in whomever these reside, there will be a teacher—whether in a school or outside one. The pervasive no-difference findings in educational research were explained as the natural outcome of the fact that the tendencies were operating in both the treatment and control groups (for example, in both large and small classes, in TV and conventional instruction, in mixed and segregated ability groups, in classrooms with textbook A and B, and so forth). The tendencies, by themselves, caused powerful learning effects that swamped any effects that could be attributed to the researcher's treatment. These spontaneous tendencies forged the defining stimulus-response learning link. They caused the stimulus to be presented, they permitted the opportunity to respond to it, and they rewarded and shaped a response to the stimulus.

The theory, like other sociobiological theories, provides a convenient base for arguing that knowledge of subject matter in the company of these tendencies will outfit a person as a teacher, especially in situations where the teacher and the pupil are a lot like each other—as they are in families and other anthropological groups.

This theory and the popular view of teaching that is implicitly based on it, however, have a number of problematical consequences for the features of modern schooling outlined above. Reliance on the theory can be expected to lead to serious pedagogical mistakes for both weak and superior students. The theory promotes an outdated mode of instruction that is not supported by the modern views of cognition and cognitive development noted above. Moreover, it provides insufficient guidance for the solution of difficult and novel problems in schooling.

When the teacher and the pupil are not alike and when the teacher has, as a result, lower expectations for the *different* pupil, the natural tendencies lead to very unfortunate consequences (Brophy and Good, 1986; Evertson, Hawley, and Zlotnick, 1985). When the teacher and the pupil have dissimilar backgrounds, we can expect that the natural teaching mechanisms that support familial instruction will not operate to benefit the student.

American teachers are a relatively homogenous set of lower-middle-class suburban white women, while the American pupil is increasingly variable with regard to every demographic feature (Howe, 1990; Choy, 1993). There are a predictable number of pedagogical mistakes novices, and regrettably some licensed teachers, make unless they have had the opportunity to practice some counter-intuitive and *unnatural* teaching techniques. For example, it is certain that well-meaning and well-read persons with good college grades will still make the following pedagogical mistakes with their pupils for whom they have low expectations, regardless of how they came to have these expectations. They will treat these pupils, not as individuals, but as a group, seat them further away and outside the classroom zone of frequent teacher-pupil interaction, look at them less, ask them low-level questions, call on them less often, give them less time to respond, give them fewer hints when they are called upon, and give them less praise and more blame than other pupils. Teachers will do all this out of a mistaken sense of kindness that is seemingly oblivious to the pedagogical harm their undisciplined actions have caused their pupils (Hawley and Rosenholtz, 1984; Murray, 1986).

This untrained and kind person, believing the pupil does not know very much, will not want to embarrass the pupil by calling on the pupil often, will ask *appropriately* easy questions when the pupil is called upon, will give fewer hints and less time when the pupil fails to respond as it would be unkind to prolong the pupil's embarrassment and so on. The professional teacher, like all professionals and in contrast with the *spontaneous* teacher, must discipline many of his or her kinder instincts and implement an equitable and disciplined professional approach to bring about high levels of achievement from those pupils for whom the teacher would otherwise have low expectations (Oakes, 1985). These professional actions are frequently counter-intuitive and as a result require practice.

A further limitation of the natural teaching regime, apart from the harm caused to weaker pupils, is that it does not take the superior pupil much beyond the kind of information that can be told and demonstrated and conforms to the stimulus-response and imitative forms of learning. While declarative knowledge can be important, the forms of knowledge that are constructed by the pupil, not merely transmitted to the pupil, are increasingly seen as key to the student's performance at the advanced levels of the disciplines (Murray, 1992; Ogle, Alsalam, and Rogers, 1991).

Along with the natural teaching techniques, there often comes a naive theory of the human mind (Heider, 1958; Baldwin, 1980). The pupil's school achievement in the naive or common sense theory is tied to four commonplace factors—ability, effort, task difficulty, and luck. With these four factors, the natural teacher can explain completely the pupil's success or failure by attributing the level of the pupil's work to his ability or effort, or to the difficulty of the school task, or to plain luck. The problem with naive theory, apart from the circularity in the four factors, is that more sophisticated theories, routinely taught in higher education, have been developed in which it can be shown that ability, to take only one example, is not fixed or stable and that it varies from moment to moment interactively with many other mental factors, not just the few in the naive theory (Baldwin, 1980; Murray, 1991b).

These naive views of how the mind works coupled with equally naive views about the nature of subject matters as received and objective truth further limit the benefits that can be expected from nonprofessional teaching that is separated from higher education. The teacher's evaluation of the pupil's correct and incorrect responses, as was noted in the *mouses/mice* example earlier, provides a telling and targeted arena for distinguishing naive and professional teachers.

A pupil's reasoning may look illogical to a naive teacher, while the educated teacher will see that the pupil's reasoning is intact, but has operated on different premises from those of the set problem. Sometimes decrements in performance, like *mouses* for *mice*, may indicate educational progress. Along similar lines, some six-year-old pupils not only maintain incorrectly that the longer row of two rows of five chips has more chips, but also maintain that the longer row must have more chips and would always have more chips. These errors occur even after the pupil has just counted the equal number of chips in each row. It happens that the error ("there *must* be more chips"), which seems the more serious error, is indicative of more developed reasoning than the error, "there are more chips." Naturally, it is very difficult for the naive or spontaneous teacher to accept any error and poor performance as a marker of progress, yet the failure to see some errors as markers of progress is another serious pedagogical mistake that stems from the untutored naive theory of teaching and learning (Bruner, 1961).

The fact that many liberal arts graduates have succeeded in meeting the expectations of the faculty in their fields of study should also not be taken as evidence that they, having studied the fundamental ideas of their field, are ready to take up work as teachers. Many of these graduates, despite their high grades, have not mastered many of the fundamental ideas of their disciplines (McDiarmid, 1992; Tyson, 1994).

There are some, of course, who hold that some level of professional knowledge should be acquired, but that a sufficient level can be reached easily and in a short period. Such a view, though a small advance in professional education for teachers, has its own problems, however. For example, on a simple reading of behavioral theory, prospective teachers will believe that positive reinforcement (or reward) is an effective and preferred way to increase the likelihood of desirable pupil behavior. Without an awareness of the important exceptions and qualifications in which rewards actually weaken a response (the *overjustification phenomenon*), teachers will make mistakes by implementing procedures that run counter to their intentions.

Teacher education is probably not warranted at the university level, however, if the teacher is held only to the standard of presenting material truthfully and clearly, to giving students an opportunity to practice, and to testing the student's grasp of the material. The modern teacher's obligation, as we have noted, is at a much higher level, a level that obligates the university and its school of education to participate in the teacher's education.

The Higher Education Response to School Reform

The modern university can accommodate and respond to many of the reform demands, primarily through thoughtful answers to the four questions above about the liberal arts components of the teacher education program. The Project 30 Alliance collaborative has undertaken a collective program to attempt to answer the questions (Project 30, 1991). These answers also entail some structural changes in the way teachers are educated.

The Holmes Group, a consortium of research universities with teacher education programs, has also charted a way for university-based schools of education to respond to the demands of school reform on higher education (see Holmes Group, 1986, 1989, 1995 for an exposition of their views on tomorrow's teachers, schools, and schools of education). In their analysis of the way higher education needs to respond to the challenges of modern school reform, the Holmes Group saw that each school of education needs to reform of each of its components—curriculum, faculty, pedagogy, students, instructional settings and groups, and partnerships.

• *Curriculum.* In its simplest terms, the new curriculum for teacher education needs to be *mapped backward,* so to speak, from the pupil's academic needs to *each* of the university's degree requirements. There must be some credible line of reasoning, in other words, that links each degree requirement in teacher education to some need a pupil has.

There should also be a frank examination of the expanded knowledge base that has developed about teaching. The nation's most able students take about four years to grasp a liberal arts education that has some added specialization in an academic discipline. Why prospective teachers, who are not high scorers generally on tests of academic aptitude (Murray, 1986), should take less time to master their teaching field and the rudiments of a liberal education is unclear. But even if there were justification in having prospective teachers study less of their fields than other students study, there are additional curriculum areas that have become important parts of the beginning teacher's academic preparation—information about technology, divergent groups of pupils, non-school factors in school achievement, and so forth. These additional areas currently push undergraduate programs at many of America's 1,179 teacher education colleges toward 150 credit hours.

There exists an additional body of knowledge that supports the teacher's reasoning about educational practice and allows the teacher to evaluate the merits of educational innovations, techniques, and policies. How should a teacher, for example, decide whether or not to adopt *ita* (the initial teaching alphabet) that regularizes spelling by having 44 *letters*, one for each of the phonemes of English?

What kind of information, to take another example, should teachers have as they reason through such policy questions as whether failing pupils should repeat a grade or be *socially* promoted to the next grade, or whether a gifted pupil should skip a grade, enter school early, be grouped separately from less gifted pupils, and so forth? Should the teacher's grades, to take still another example, be expected to follow a normal distribution or some other pattern? Should pupils use calculators in their arithmetic lessons and homework? What should the teacher have studied and experienced to avoid making mistakes in answering these questions?

Just on the arithmetic of it, an honest teacher education program (that is, one that provides mastery and understanding of the teaching field, liberal and general education, educational theory and research, modern pedagogical knowledge, and effective clinical practice) will take more time than is available in the four-year 120-credit hour undergraduate program.

Apart from the amount of new information that is available for teachers to study, there is a need, in response to the third question above, for a qualitatively different kind of discipline of pedagogy, a graduate-level discipline. The criteria for a firm distinction between undergraduate and graduate education are, of course, contested and elusive. It is generally accepted, however, that the study of a subject is at the graduate level if it is qualitatively transformed by its connection to some set of prerequisite studies. The study of statistics, for example, can involve little more than the acquisition of algorithms, computer programs, and graphical representations, but it is qualitatively different when it is formulated algebraically, and different again when it is formulated in the calculus.

How can the study of pedagogy be justified at the graduate level? How could it be qualitatively different from the study of pedagogy as it is currently found at the undergraduate level? When a physics teacher employs a hydraulic analogy to clarify electric current (that is, electricity behaves like water in pipes), what kind of knowledge is the analogy? It is not part of physics insofar as the physical account of electricity does not require the analogy, yet the analogy is dependent upon an understanding of physics. What is the source of the analogy; from what discipline does it spring? Is it even a good short-term or long-term way to think about electric current? From what source do expert teachers construct a telling example, metaphor, analogy, or expression for a concept for a particular student in a particular setting? This kind of knowledge, as we noted in the subtraction algorithm example above, is not found in the discipline nor is it found in the study of instructional strategies like direct instruction, cooperative learning, maieutic teaching, process teaching, reciprocal teaching, and so forth.

This kind of knowledge is dependent upon both the academic discipline and education, but it is different from each and derived from another as yet unspecified source. As it is qualitatively different from its progenitors, it is properly thought of as graduate-level study.

It is sufficient for the argument about the new teacher education curriculum to show that there is a kind of understanding, indispensable to the teacher's art, that merits graduate-level status insofar as it is qualitatively different from its prerequisites and dependent upon them. It is a kind of understanding that makes explicit what is otherwise the tacit knowledge of experts. It is the kind of knowledge that exists uniquely in higher education even though its codification has just developed. Finally, it is the kind of knowledge that is essential for the new teacher who will implement the features of the modern school, the school that is uncompromising in its goal that all its pupils will understand their lessons.

• *Faculty.* The Holmes Group, and other higher education reformers, have called for the invention, not just of a new discipline of academic teacher education, but of a new kind of faculty member— a person who is equally at home in the university and in the public school classroom. A clinical professor, for want of a better term, is needed, who can show and do what education professors would otherwise be lecturing about in university classes on pedagogy. Clinical professors of pedagogy could originate and be developed from two directions—from the university faculty and from the public school faculty. It follows that the clinical faculty would practice a pedagogy that had the features of the modern school discussed at the outset of this chapter. They would practice what they preached, in other words.

• *Instructional settings.* In *Tomorrow's Schools,* the Holmes Group (1989) made the case for a new kind of public school that would serve teacher education the way teaching hospitals serve medical education. They called these schools *professional development schools* (PDSs) and saw that part of the PDS mission was to be the site for as much of the prospective teacher's education as could be managed (see also Petrie, 1995, for further explication of the issues involved in the PDS).

• *Instructional arrangement.* One of the more far reaching of the Holmes Group proposals for restructuring teacher education, apart from the invention of the PDS, is the notion that educators should be educated as they would function. The view that teachers, counselors, school psychologists, curriculum specialists, and administrators should work in relative isolation of each other is no longer held, if it ever was. Educational scholarship insistently demonstrates the value of a team approach to the school's problems, and it would follow that future educators, despite their delineated roles and licenses, should work as members of the same team and be educated with that outcome in mind.

As much of the curriculum as possible should be common to each of the professional roles and as much of the instructional activity should be in common also in the restructured school of education. The recommendation is based upon more than the efficacy of team-based problem solutions. It is based also on the fact that each of the professional education roles—teacher, counselor, administrator, etc.—is legitimized by its unique hypotheses and suppositions about the underlying causes of pupil performance. When the pupil habitually fails to learn his lessons, each professional specialist offers its own group's explanation. The special educator sees the pupil's chronic failure as a matter of an inappropriate curriculum or pedagogy, the counselor sees the problem as a matter of the pupil's self-esteem or anxiety over non-school issues, the school psychologist often sees the problem in terms of the pupil's tested ability, the administrator may see the difficulty in terms of the school's organization or pupil grouping or promotion policies, and so on. The point is that each specialist, like the blind discovering the elephant, has an explanation of the pupil's problem that could benefit from the others' perspectives. The education of each should be arranged so that as often as possible each has the opportunity to validate and confirm the limitations of his or her own guild's perspectives against the challenge of other educational specialist's interpretations of the same events.

• *Students.* Nearly every reform group has seen the need to expand the composition of the cohort of professional educators to include members of several underrepresented groups. Special efforts are called for, like the Holmes Scholar initiative to recruit people of color into the ranks of the next generation of teacher educators. Currently, there are stark underrepresentations in professional education of people of color, men and women in selected teaching fields and roles, and overrepresentations of low scorers on academic measures of prior accomplishment everywhere in the system.

• *Partnerships*. Finally, the members of the Holmes Group, after a decade of making uneven progress in the reform of teacher education, concluded that schools of education cannot bring about the reforms cited throughout this chapter by themselves. (In 1995, the Holmes Group restructured its organization into the Holmes Partnership, an organization of universities, public schools, and national professional organizations. Universities can no longer be members of the organization. They must form a partnership with local public schools or districts and that partnership is the member of the Holmes Partnership.) Initially, they saw, like the members of the Project 30 Alliance and others, that many of the weaknesses in teacher education could be addressed by strengthening the links between the faculty in the school of education and the faculty in the rest of the university. Certainly, the reform of the major portion of the teacher education degree entails a partnership between education and liberal arts faculty.

The complete reform of the schools of education, however, requires more than that, and the invention of the PDS has made it clear that the links to the fields of professional practice need strengthening also. The need for partnerships between schools of education and the rest of the university and the educational professions is far more than a device for political advantage, although it is surely that. The needs of the new school of education for a new curriculum, faculty, instructional site, and so forth also require the intellectual contributions of higher education *and* the profession. Only then will teaching take its place as one of the learned professions that merits, like the other learned professions, the unwavering investment of higher education in it. For that investment to matter, however, higher education has to provide better answers to the questions the public and the schools ask of it and its schools of education.

Conclusion

Although higher education clearly needs to alter many aspects of itself to meet the needs of tomorrow's teachers and tomorrow's schools, there are other aspects of the public schooling reform movements that speak to the reform of higher education. In the spring of 1983, the secretary of education's National Commission on Excellence in Education, after eighteen months of study, reported that due to a rising tide of mediocrity the quality of American schooling had eroded over the prior two decades to a point that threatened the very future of the nation and its people. The nation, the commission concluded, was at risk, and so by implication were the nation's colleges and universities. They were at risk not simply because the students in colleges and universities were so recently students in the afflicted high schools, but because the same forces that had eroded the public schools operated as well in the colleges and universities (Murray, 1985). The lessons from the 1983 reports, and the more than 160 subsequent national and state reports that echoed the findings of the National Commission, were virtually the same for the colleges and the public schools. Thus, the challenges for higher education are doubly difficult, as they require general reform as well as the reforms that are particular to teacher education.

References

Baldwin, A. *Theories of Child Development.* (2nd ed.) New York: John Wiley, 1980.

Ball, D. "The Mathematical Understandings That Preservice Teachers Bring to Teacher Education." *Elementary School Journal,* 1990, 90, 449–466.

Ball, D. "Teaching Mathematics for Understanding: What Do Teachers Need to Know About Subject Matter?" In M. Kennedy (ed.), *Teaching Academic Subjects to Diverse Learners.* New York: Teachers College Press, 1991.

Banks, J. "The Canon Debate, Knowledge Construction, and Multicultural Education." *Educational Researcher,* 1993, 22(5), 4–14.

Blits, J. "The Search for Ends: Liberal Education and the Modern University." In J. Blits (ed.), *The American University.* Buffalo, N.Y.: Prometheus Books, 1985.

Brophy, J., and Good, T. "Teacher Behavior and Student Achievement." In M. Wittrock (ed.), *Handbook of Research on Teaching.* (3rd ed.) New York: Macmillan, 1986.

Bruner, J. *The Process of Education.* Cambridge, Mass.: Harvard University Press, 1961.

Choy, S., and others. *America's Teachers: Profile of a Profession*. Washington, D.C.: National Center for Education Statistics, 1993.

Evertson, C., Hawley, W., and Zlotnick, M. "Making a Difference in Educational Quality Through Teacher Education." *Journal of Teacher Education*, 1985, 36(3), 2–12.

Gardner, H. *The Unschooled Mind: How Children Think and How Schools Should Teach*. New York: Basic Books, 1991.

Guthrie, R. *Even the Rat Was White: A Historical View of Psychology*. New York: HarperCollins, 1976.

Hawley, W., and Rosenholtz, S. "Good Schools: What Research Says About Improving Student Achievement." *Peabody Journal of Education*, 1984, 61(4).

Heider, F. *The Psychology of Interpersonal Relations*. New York: Wiley, 1958.

Holmes Group. *Tomorrow's Teachers: A Report of the Holmes Group*. East Lansing, Mich.: Holmes Group, 1986.

Holmes Group. *Tomorrow's Schools*. East Lansing, Mich.: Holmes Group, 1989.

Holmes Group. *Tomorrow's School of Education*. East Lansing, Mich.: Holmes Group, 1995.

Howe, H. "Thinking About the Forgotten Half." *Teachers College Record*, 1990, 92, 293–305.

Kamii, C. *Young Children Continue to Reinvent Arithmetic-2nd Grade*. New York: Teachers College Press, 1989.

Kennedy, M. M. (ed.). *Teaching Academic Subjects to Diverse Learners*. New York: Teachers College Press, 1991.

McDiarmid, G. W. "The Liberal Arts: Will More Result in Better Subject Matter Understanding?" *Theory into Practice*, 1990, 29(1), 21–29.

McDiarmid, G. W. *The Arts and Sciences as Preparation for Teaching*. Issue Paper 92–3. East Lansing, Mich.: National Center for Research on Teacher Learning, 1992.

Murray, F. "The Pedagogical Adequacy of Children's Conservation Explanations." *Journal of Educational Psychology*, 1982, 74(5), 656–659.

Murray, F. "Paradoxes of a University at Risk." In J. Blits (ed.), *The American University*. Buffalo, N.Y.: Prometheus Books, 1985.

Murray, F. "Teacher Education." *Change*, Sept./Oct. 1986, pp. 18–21.

Murray, F. "Alternative Conceptions of Academic Knowledge for Prospective Elementary Teachers." In M. Pugach, H. Barnes, and L. Beckum (eds.), *Changing the Practices of Teacher Education: The Role of the Knowledge Base*. Washington, D.C.: American Association of Colleges for Teacher Education, 1991a.

Murray, F. "Questions a Satisfying Developmental Theory Would Answer: The Scope of a Complete Explanation of Developmental Phenomena." In H. Reese (ed.), *Advances in Child Development and Behavior*. Vol. 23. New York: Academic Press, 1991b.

Murray, F. "Restructuring and Constructivism: The Development of American Educational Reform." In H. Beilin and P. Pufall (eds.), *Piaget's Theory: Prospects and Possibilities*. Hillsdale, N.J.: Erlbaum, 1992.

Murray, F., and Fallon, D. *The Reform of Teacher Education for the 21st Century: Project 30 Year One Report*. Newark: University of Delaware, 1989.

Murray, F., and Johnson, P. "A Note on Using Curriculum Models in Analyzing the Child's Concept of Weight." *Journal of Research in Science Teaching*, 1970, 7, 377–381.

Murray, F., and Johnson, P. "Relevant and Some Irrelevant Factors in the Child's Concept of Weight." *Journal of Educational Psychology*, 1975, 67, 705–711.

Murray, F., and Markessini, J. "A Semantic Basis of Nonconservation of Weight." *Psychological Record*, 1982, 32, 375–379.

Oakes, J. *Keeping Track: How Schools Structure Inequality*. New Haven, Conn.: Yale University Press, 1985.

Ogle, L., Alsalam, N., and Rogers, G. *The Condition of Education 1991*. Washington, D.C.: National Center for Education Statistics, 1991.

Petrie, H. *Professionalization, Partnership, and Power: Building Professional Development Schools*. Albany: State University of New York Press, 1995.

Project 30. *Project 30 Year Two Report: Institutional Accomplishments*. Newark: University of Delaware, 1991.

Scardamalia, M., and Bereiter, C. "Higher Levels of Agency for Children in Knowledge Building: A Challenge for the Design of New Knowledge Media." *Journal of the Learning Sciences*, 1991, 1, 37–68.

Sheingold, K. "Restructuring for Learning with Technology: The Potential for Synergy." *Phi Delta Kappan*, Sept. 1991, 73, 17–27.

Shulman, L. "Those Who Understand: Knowledge Growth in Teaching." *Educational Researcher*, 1986, 15(2), 4–14.

Shulman, L. "Knowledge and Teaching: Foundations of the New Reform." *Harvard Educational Review*, 1987, 57(1), 1–22.

Siegler, R. "Developmental Sequences Within and Between Concepts." *Monographs of the Society for Research in Child Development*, 1981, 46(189).

Stephens, J. M. *The Process of Schooling: A Psychological Examination*. Austin, Tex.: Holt, Rinehart and Winston, 1967.

Tyson, H. *Who Will Teach the Children? Progress and Resistance in Teacher Education*. San Francisco: Jossey-Bass, 1994.

Chapter Six

School Improvement and Higher Education

David K. Cohen

Reformers have been trying to promote intellectually more demanding public school instruction since the mid-1980s, and researchers have been trying to understand the reforms and their effects since then. As part of that effort I have seen many significant changes in instruction, but I am troubled by the intellectually drab and superficial quality of much that my colleagues and I see and hear.[1] I am especially troubled because it seems plain that most students in the classrooms that we observe could do more thoughtful work, and that most teachers are quite bright enough to help them do it.

One reason that students do not do a better job is that their teachers do not invite it, and one reason that teachers do not invite it is that they have little idea of what much better instruction might be. One reason for that is that the colleges and universities they attended did not offer an education that would have helped them to know what much better instruction would look like, and how they might achieve it. Higher education is not the only source of intellectually drab schoolwork. Schools and school districts share a good deal of the responsibility, as do parents, politicians, and the public. I pursue the connections between higher and

This chapter has been improved by discussion by members of the Pew Forum on Education Reform, for which it was initially written. Professor Constance Cook at the University of Michigan and Michael Timpane of the Carnegie Foundation for the Advancement of Teaching also had many helpful suggestions.

lower education here in part because so much commentary has focused elsewhere.

Instruction and Higher Education

Most colleges and universities do not offer students many opportunities to learn about the sort of intellectually ambitious instruction that reformers want to see in the lower schools. On the contrary, they offer rich opportunities for intending teachers to learn the sorts of instruction that reformers think should be discouraged. There are some important exceptions: A handful of special institutions have actively supported good teaching for decades, as have a few special programs within larger institutions, and of course there are outstanding teachers scattered throughout the system. In addition, since the early 1970s quite a few universities report that they have established programs or centers that offer assistance in the improvement of instruction. Since the early 1980s there has been an appreciable increase in worry and commentary about the quality of college and university instruction and efforts to improve teaching (Shulman, 1993).

Despite these encouraging developments, those who study higher education report that most instruction is didactic and dull (McKeatchie, Pintrich, Lin, and Smith, 1986). Lectures and recitation dominate. Multiple choice tests are the rule even in many of the "better" universities. Many students reach their junior or senior year without ever having been asked what they thought about an issue, or how they would frame a problem. Many graduate from college without ever writing an essay and receiving comments on it from a professor, let alone rewriting it and receiving more comments from the same professor. Universities have taken some steps to improve instruction, including establishing centers devoted to the evaluation and improvement of instruction, but interviews with staffers at several centers reveal that few professors avail themselves of their services, save course evaluation, which often is mandatory. The center staff report that they work chiefly with graduate teaching assistants and beginning junior faculty. In addition, though universities have announced hundreds of departmental efforts to improve colleagueship and instruction, Massey, Wilger, and Colbeck (1994) report that in a study of academic departments in twenty colleges and universities, respondents seldom reported the "substantial discussions necessary to improve undergraduate education."

This unfortunate situation is not the work of poorly educated faculty. It holds even for the great research universities, whose faculty are very well educated. There are some fine teachers at these places, and nearly all know the subjects that they teach very well— unlike many teachers in the lower schools. But deep knowledge of a subject is only one element of good academic instruction. To teach well one also must understand how novices think about physics, math, or history, and know how to represent such subjects in ways that will give novices access to them. Relatively few academics give much attention to such matters.

Indeed, in a sense, well-educated faculty get in the way of good teaching. Both knowledge and ideas about the disciplines have been changing. Being well-educated has less and less to do with broad learning within a discipline and more and more to do with mastering a relatively narrow sub-disciplinary specialty. The undergraduate course structure reflects that specialization. As a result, fewer professors teach in ways that reflect a grasp of the large intellectual structure of their discipline or profession, partly because their own knowledge is quite specialized and partly because their departmental curricula are organized around specialized courses that reflect the changing intellectual substructure of their fields. Moreover, the better the university, the more likely it is that professors will see undergraduate courses as recruiting opportunities for disciplinary majors and applicants to graduate school, rather than as occasions for general education. In mathematics and the sciences especially, faculty see undergraduate courses as the academic equivalent of the 440 high hurdles: The point is to identify those students who are talented enough for specialized graduate work, and to wash out the rest (Shulman, 1993). Hence more and more instruction in arts and sciences faculties seems less suitable for students who wish to major in a field so as to become thoughtful teachers in the schools below, rather than going on for a specialized and research-oriented Ph.D. Those who propose to use higher education to improve academic instruction in the lower schools therefore must come to terms with a paradox: Knowledge of a discipline is essential to good academic instruction, but the continuing specialized redefinition of the disciplines and the role that undergraduate teaching plays in disciplinary recruitment increasingly impede the capacity of disciplinary scholars to offer such instruction. This potent effect of disciplinary research on instruction is little noticed in discussions of reform in the lower schools.

Perhaps the most important consequence of this situation, for those interested in the reform of public education, is that very few potential teachers, parents, and taxpayers get much college or university experience with the sort of teaching and learning that they wish to promote in elementary and secondary schools. Unlike most other sorts of work that require formal training or extended apprenticeships, teachers, parents, and citizens learn a great deal about teaching and how it is done by having been students. That is unique: No one learns anything of consequence about how to fly an airplane by traveling as a passenger, and we learn very little about how to practice medicine or dentistry from our service as patients. But nearly everyone learns a great deal about teaching through long careers as students (Lortie, 1975). Researchers increasingly identify that learning as a key barrier to dramatic change in teaching. Hence parents and taxpayers-to-be, who will decide whether or not to support reform in many state and local elections in the coming years, are poorly informed about what good and serious instruction looks like, what it takes to do it, and why it can be worthwhile. They also are poorly informed about why it is likely to take a long and extraordinary effort to change teaching in K–12 schools, because they never have been part of a serious effort to do so. Nearly everyone in the United States, including teachers-to-be and experienced teachers, is poorly informed about the instruction that reformers want schools to offer, about how to offer it, and about why it might be worth their effort.

As one considers the prospects for instructional reform in elementary and secondary schools, these broad political consequences of college and university instruction are no less troubling than the narrower consequences in pedagogy. Yet analysts and reformers interested in better teaching and learning in the schools have been nearly silent on how instruction in higher education bears on instruction in the schools. Though it is encouraging that the major universities are dotted with efforts to improve courses, I have found no evidence of any larger agenda for instructional change in higher education, let alone something that resembles the beginning of a movement for such change.

Approaches to Reform

We can learn more about the issues by considering some recent proposals to improve public education by changing higher education.

Improve Professionalism in Teacher Education

One relatively popular idea has been to make schools and departments of education more professional, an idea that a collection of U.S. education schools called the Holmes Group has vigorously advocated. Holmes leaders argue that there will not be better schools without better teachers, and that better teachers will need much more professional education. In the Holmes program, better teachers would know more about teaching, both from studying research and from more extended clinical teacher education, and would have studied the subjects they are to teach much more deeply.

The Holmes proposals center on how to change university education so as to produce such teachers. Many of the proposals focus on changes in education curricula, including much more work in schools for intending teachers and the creation of Professional Development Schools in which novices could learn their trade under the supervision of first-class practitioners. Improved teacher education that is somehow rooted in practice seems an excellent idea, but one must bear in mind that schools of education are only a small bit of the higher education enterprise. Intending elementary teachers take only one-quarter or one-third of their undergraduate coursework in education schools or departments, and intending high school teachers typically take much less. The instructional problems of higher education reside chiefly in faculties of arts and sciences, because that is where most courses are offered and taken and where most influence over instruction resides.

The Holmes proposals recognize that, for they propose to require intending elementary teachers to be subject-matter majors in arts and sciences departments, not education majors. Deeper knowledge of the subjects they will teach also seems essential, but the notion that more instruction in arts and science departments will greatly improve the education of intending teachers should give anyone familiar with higher education pause. If elementary teachers-to-be learn more math, science, and literature, they will learn them principally in math, science, and English departments. That would be a real gain in some university courses and departments and in a handful of small colleges that are oriented to undergraduate teaching. But research on instruction in higher education implies that in most universities, where most teachers are educated, such additional learning typically would be marked by intellectual fragmentation and poor pedagogy. Though intending teachers need more disciplinary knowledge, they may not profit greatly from the disciplinary knowledge that most would be taught in the arts and sciences courses that most colleges and universities would offer them.

Those who are troubled by this assertion should consider high schools. One legacy of James Conant's reforms in the 1950s and 1960s was that high school teachers' higher education became the responsibility of disciplinary departments rather than education schools. Intending secondary teachers had to major in an academic discipline and to take only two or three education courses. As a result, they know much more in their disciplines than elementary teachers, but their pedagogy is no better—in fact, observers report that teaching in U.S. high schools is even more drab than in elementary schools (Powell, Farrar, and Cohen, 1985).

Despite this, teaching in education schools and departments could be much improved, for better coursework could boost intending teachers' understanding of disciplinary knowledge. In mathematics, for instance, if education methods courses were taught by people who were sophisticated teachers of children and deeply knowledgeable about math, that would improve on many current methods courses, and would greatly improve on most of the math department courses that intending teachers take. But it would not be easy to accomplish even such a modest reform. Many math methods teachers have not taught children for decades, and if their undergraduate teaching is any indicator, their pedagogy is quite routine. For these faculty members to learn how to teach children well, and then to learn how to import that knowledge and skill into their methods classes, would not be easy.

Even if those problems were solved tomorrow, there still would be larger ones to solve the day after. Just to continue the example, most education schools offer a single, one-semester math methods course and do not have room in the curriculum to offer two. That is partly because of state and professional requirements that arise outside education schools, but it also is the result of requirements inside them. Students must also take courses in learning psychology, history, sociology, reading, and other subjects. Just as the education curriculum is a modest part of intending teachers' entire curriculum, learning about disciplinary-based pedagogy is an even more modest part of the education curriculum. So while the education school curriculum has much room to improve, it would not be sensible either to expect such improvement to replace bad disciplinary coursework offered elsewhere on campus, to repair the pedagogical damage that it does, or to think that major improvement would be possible without a fundamental overhaul of the curriculum in education schools.

A further limit on the likely influence of education school reforms is that they enroll only education students. Even if all U.S. education schools and departments had dramatically improved curricula today, the effect tomorrow on what "educated" Americans learn about teaching and learning would be nil because few of those Americans take courses in education schools. That is no reason to avoid improving curriculum and instruction in education schools, but we should be clear about what to expect. Major reforms in the education schools' curriculum could modestly improve what teachers know and how they teach, and that in turn could have modest effects on the quality of teaching and learning in the lower schools. But as long as higher education is carved up and conducted as it now is, education school reform by itself is unlikely to be a major force in the reform of public education.

Stiffen Admission Standards

A second proposal has been to make college entrance much more difficult. Reformers claim that tough standards for entry above would improve the incentives for good work in the schools below, and that better admission standards to the academy would improve work within it. Given the immense variation in quality among institutions of higher education, and the very weak standards of admission at many such places, it is difficult to argue with efforts to improve admission standards, but it is not self-evident that they would have the desired effects. Consider this thought experiment: We suddenly cause all 2,000 to 3,000 odd institutions of higher education to have the same stiff admission standards, well-educated faculty, and disciplinary curricula as the top thirty or forty colleges and universities. Is it reasonable to expect a dramatic improvement in instruction either within the formerly less selective institutions or in the schools below? There certainly would be at least an initial dramatic decrease in admissions to higher education, a corresponding dramatic increase in unhappiness among rejected high school seniors and juniors and their parents and teachers, and even greater unhappiness among administrators and faculty at institutions that might be put out of business by the decline in acceptable applicants. There also would be greatly increased pressure on higher education to weaken the new standards, or the appearance of new colleges and universities eager to accept these newly unhappy and rejected applicants, or both. In a weakly regulated market, stiff standards might be no match for clients eager to pay for a relaxed college and university experience. The history of episodic efforts to stiffen standards of work in public schools suggests that even in a highly regulated government enterprise, client resistance can have a crippling effect.

But suppose that the higher standards were kept in place, against all precedent in American educational history, and that new institutions catering to those in search of low standards were kept from entering the market. Would there not be a dramatic improvement in college and university instruction?

Improving the content of college, university, and high school courses would improve the content of students' work, which would be quite desirable, but there is no reason to expect that either teachers' pedagogy or students' understanding would change. One reason for this view arises from the dynamics of teaching: Teachers who have highly selected and motivated students can get a decent instructional result for a more modest effort than their otherwise equally capable colleagues who teach in much less selective places. It is, after all, quite a bit easier to teach respectably with students who are intent on doing well, who are well educated, and who know how to do well in school than with students who wished they were at a party or a football game, who are not well educated, and who do not know how to do good work. So if we imagine that all professors suddenly had only highly selected and motivated students, and if we imagine that professors are no less rational than other humans, then we should not suppose that raising admission standards to their institutions would much increase either their efforts to understand students' thinking or to improve their pedagogy. That seems especially plausible when we consider that professors in selective universities have research and other professional work that they value at least as much as teaching.

Another reason to expect change chiefly in the content of instruction arises from recent research. Two recent studies report that the pedagogy in highly esteemed secondary schools was nothing to write home about (Powell, Farrar, and Cohen, 1985; Bryk, Lee, and Holland, 1993). Even in these unusual schools, teaching looked very much like the lectures, recitation, seatwork and other things that reformers deplore in much lesser schools. But very conventional teaching worked in such schools, partly because teachers did not have to work classroom miracles to help their students do well; these schools had many other ways to help teachers and students do well. The schools were distinguished by collegial relations among faculty, an ethic of caring for students, control over admissions and expulsion, few enough students that teachers and administrators could know and care for them, and students who all took much of the curriculum in common and were expected to do serious academic work. Classroom teaching could be uninspired because in such relatively encouraging circumstances, it did not need to be anything but serious to get good results.

A third reason to expect no more than improved content from stiffer admission standards is historical—we already tried it with Conant's reforms of secondary school teaching. Despite considerable improvement in high school teachers' subject matter knowledge since the late 1950s there have been no observed improvements in pedagogy. By all accounts high school teaching is still drab in the same ways as it was thirty years ago (Powell, Farrar, and Cohen, 1985, ch. 5).

Strong admission standards and improved academic content are very important, and the absence of serious admission standards in all but a small subsector of U.S. higher education is one reason that intellectually demanding work is so uncommon in the lower schools. Nonetheless, admission standards are not an instructional cure-all. There is, for example, no evidence that undergraduate teaching is any better at highly selective Harvard than at somewhat less selective University of Wisconsin. For a long time, Michigan State University, which is much less selective than Wisconsin, was said to have better undergraduate instruction than many much more selective universities. The reasons offered for such differences have more to do with institutional culture and purpose than with selectivity—witness the reputation for fine teaching that has grown up around Miami-Dade Community College and other entirely unselective institutions. If we want simply to improve the level of academic effort in the upper and lower schools, then stiffening standards for admission to higher education (and to jobs, for high school leavers) would be reasonable, if we could figure out how to do it without fomenting a revolt, or closing down hundreds or thousands of colleges and universities, or being defeated by the rapid emergence of new institutions catering to the low standards market. If we want to improve instruction, students' understanding, and their capacity as independent problem solvers, then we need to consider measures that would directly address those features of teaching and learning that go beyond admission standards and course content.

Strengthen Incentives for Teaching

A third line of thought about reform is that the reason for weak college and university teaching is weak incentives for good teaching. Colleges and universities that want to promote more rich and thoughtful work in lower schools by teaching future citizens to appreciate it and teachers how to do it should reward good and penalize bad teaching. If the quality of teaching weighed heavily in decisions about hiring, promotion, and tenure, then college and university teaching would improve.

That idea seems plausible, partly because the incentives for good teaching are weak in U.S. colleges and universities, and they sometimes seem to get weaker as the institutions get stronger. It seems reasonable to suppose therefore that more potent incentives for good teaching would help, but such incentives are easier to discuss than to change. One key problem is that incentives for research-oriented college and university faculty are shaped less by the institutions in which they work than by disciplines that span institutions of higher education. When faculty members focus more on research than teaching they choose to attend to work that "contributes to the discipline" rather than to learners in a specific institution. Teaching sociology or chemistry very well is valued by many university faculty members and administrators, but it is rarely counted as a contribution to those disciplines, even by those who value it. Great teachers—like Georg Polya—are sometimes applauded, but one reason that Polya was recognized for his teaching even among mathematicians was that he wrote about it in ways that were cogent, scholarly, and deeply connected to mathematical thought. Another was that he continued to be a productive research mathematician.

When reformers propose to change incentives for teaching, they attend to university rather than disciplinary priorities, and the two are far from identical. Hiring, promotion, and tenure are the key labor-force decisions made in universities and colleges, but these decisions are not made by executives but by the workers, an unprecedented practice in American labor relations. Higher education managers rely on the workers' judgment—that is, the decisions of disciplinary faculty committees—and those judgments tend to focus on disciplinary concerns such as the significance of candidates' research, the quality and quantity of their research, their promise as researchers, and their service to the discipline or profession. Hence managers and institutions depend on disciplines that cut across institutional boundaries. Academic departments do not hire the economists, political scientists, sociologists, or psychologists that deans and provosts want, unless committees of disciplinary faculty concur. Deans and provosts ordinarily do not even have articulate wants for hiring within disciplinary departments, aside for preferences for women or members of minority groups, or to hire either stars or younger and less expensive candidates. University managers typically do no more than choose among or disapprove disciplinary nominations made by disciplinary faculty.

This approach to job decisions has grave liabilities. Hiring and promotion decisions have tended to transmit the complexion and gender composition of the disciplines, and they have given teaching modest weight at best. Reports on teaching now are often considered in these decisions, but they are rarely considered in the same detail or with the same seriousness as disciplinary concerns. Nor is the evidence on teaching given anything approaching equivalent weight to evidence on research and publication. But given the astonishing explosion and specialization of knowledge in the last century, it is difficult to imagine a better way to make decisions about faculty. As a student of public education who teaches at a school of education and cares about improved instruction, I want hiring and tenure decisions to give greater weight to teaching, but as a faculty member in a leading research university I want those decisions to be well informed, and no one is as well-informed in these matters as the disciplinary workers.

In addition, even if higher education institutions strengthened the incentives for good teaching, that would be unlikely to have a major effect on decisions about hiring, promotion, and tenure. One reason is cognitive and organizational: the disciplines are so crucial to the intellectual and social structure of universities that deans, provosts, and faculty committees would be unlikely even to imagine viable ways to strengthen incentives for teaching that would substantially weaken disciplinary values such as research. Imagination would fail even if courage did not. It seems much more likely that deans, provosts, and faculty committees would devise marginally stronger incentives for teaching that would not weaken incentives for research and service to the discipline. Such changes would be a significant but modest improvement.

Another reason to expect only modest improvement in response to stronger incentives for teaching arises from the competitive nature of American higher education. University and college executives worry about their institutions' positions and reputations, and regularly try to maintain or improve them. To do so they usually focus on athletic programs, tuition, and the quality of faculty and students. One standard way to maintain or improve institutional quality is to recruit better faculty, and in most cases that means better disciplinary researchers. As long as the enterprise is so competitive and the disciplines so central, it is difficult to see how the weight of disciplinary judgments about quality could be greatly reduced. If that is so, increased incentives for good teaching would have only modest effects.

Someone will say that this situation could easily be changed if only higher education gave more weight to judgments about pedagogical quality—but that is vastly more easily said than done, even if we ignore the disciplines. The central problem is that colleges and universities lack a rich body of knowledge about the nature of good teaching, they lack shared values about what is good in good teaching, and they lack experience in making important career decisions based on judgments that distinguish good from ordinary or poor teaching. These lacks are important, because in order to take teaching into account in significant decisions, higher education would need professionally and politically defensible ways to do so. That would require deep knowledge about teaching quality, considerable agreement on standards and values, and defensible decision-making procedures. At the moment there are no defensible standards for discriminating among the varieties and quality of teaching, even though there are some ideas, some research, and some unanalyzed experience. Indeed, there is not even agreement on what the anchors for standards of teaching would be. Would standards be tied to results—that is, students' learning? If so, to what results: simple achievement tests? Essay exams? Oral examinations? Some combination of these? What university would agree to achievement testing of students, let alone to using student scores to decide about faculty? Would standards depend instead on observed pedagogical process, and if so, who would observe, and what elements of instructional process would be observed? How would such observation of pedagogy be validated, if not with reference to students' learning?

The United States being a divided and argumentative society, the lack of defensible answers to these questions makes one thing nearly certain: Efforts to give much greater weight to teaching would be likely to provoke more lawsuits and related troubles than improved teaching. These issues have not been settled for teachers in the lower schools despite nearly a century of extensive research, extended controversy, and repeated efforts to discern and establish standards for judging the quality of teaching. Very few public schools and school systems try to make more than the most rudimentary judgments about this matter, despite many more efforts. Who imagines that things would be easier in universities, where Americans are no less divided and much better at argument?

Even if those problems were solved, stronger incentives for teaching still would be far from sufficient to get college and university teachers to improve their work dramatically. Incentives alone would be a sensible course of action only if teachers knew how to do the things that would be rewarded, but did not do them because other things were more highly rewarded or more fiercely punished; or if teachers did not know how to teach well but could relatively easily and conveniently learn to do the things that would be rewarded, and not to do the things that would be punished. In the first case, changed incentives could shift the balance from one sort of known practice to another, whereas in the second, incentives could encourage practitioners to learn a new practice quickly while unlearning an old one.

Unfortunately, neither of these conditions obtain in most American colleges and universities. Dull and didactic teaching cannot be principally explained by teachers choosing not to do what they know how to do well because the incentives for research are stronger. Nor is there easily available knowledge about how to learn to teach well. Research on teaching strongly suggests that it is complicated and difficult to learn to teach in ways that respect students' thinking, that open disciplinary and professional material up to students' understanding, and that create rich opportunities for students to consider and reconsider their ideas (Cohen, McLaughlin, and Talbert, 1993). Few institutions of higher education have the educational resources needed to help many professors learn to teach differently, though a few have the resources to help a few instructors to begin to learn.

Consider, by way of example, one of the difficulties of learning to teach in ways that respect students' thinking and open disciplinary knowledge to their understanding. On one hand, to become a good professor is to learn to master a discipline, but on the other, as they do so most professors forget or bypass all those features of novice performance that they would need to appreciate in order to teach in ways that were sensitive to students' thinking. In disciplines, as in other practices, it becomes more difficult to recreate and appreciate novice performance as one becomes more accomplished (Cohen, 1996b). Few good swimmers could spontaneously reproduce their earlier incompetence, paddling as though incapable of swimming and then recreating their progress toward expert performance. Anyone can thrash and choke, but few decent swimmers could recapture the key difficulties that they encountered and then reenact the crucial steps in their learning, let alone use that recaptured knowledge to inform their work as swimming teachers. For to learn to swim well is to lose the bad habits, poor attitudes, and awkwardness of beginners and poor swimmers. Such losses are a crucial part of learning—indeed, learning to swim well could not occur without massive forgetting. That is not unique to swimming. The more polished our performances become in any realm, the less we remember how we did things less capably. If we did not forget novice habits, ideas, and attitudes as we learned more, every new performance would be a struggle to learn everything all over again. Psychologists commonly think about learning as a matter of adding something new, but what is subtracted is no less important. If we did not forget most elements of novice performance, life and learning would be endless repetitions. Little ever would be solidly achieved because little would be left behind. All learners would be Sisyphus.[2]

If such strategic forgetting advances learning, it inhibits good teaching. Like everyone else, most teachers have forgotten many experiences that might help them to build bridges back to those they try to teach. Like everyone else, they are encouraged to forget in part by the allure of polished performance. For to be knowledgeable and skillful is to produce polished work. The greater one's mastery, the more elegant and efficient one's performance. Mastery is something to be cherished, no less in smooth driving over a winding road than in writing a historical essay or solving a physics problem. One reason that math teachers work problems at the board as cleanly as they can is that mathematicians see elegance as a mark of good work. Stumbling through problems piecemeal seems clumsy, even though that is what mathematicians usually do on the way to cracking them. Similarly, many English teachers read from Twain or Hemingway's best stories rather than some messy early draft because that is the sort of writing they hope students will strive to produce and appreciate. What could be more reasonable than to launch such examples toward learners?

When teachers launch polished, finished knowledge toward learners, their work embodies crucial elements of the high culture and aspirations of a practice, be it physics or violin playing. Such finished performances express high achievement and are an essential means of communication among accomplished practitioners. In addition, such knowledge is essential for good teaching, for if teachers did not know what polished work was like, they could hardly know what they want to achieve, nor could they help students to head in a fruitful direction. Without the knowledge and skill that such performances embody, teachers could never recognize signs of competent performance, inventiveness, insight, or misunderstanding among learners. Despite all this, finished knowledge and appreciation of polished performance also can inhibit the cultivation of a practice of teaching, for they regularly blind teachers to how knowledge might be unpacked for learners' benefit.

Hence there are many good reasons that intellectually accomplished professors find it difficult to teach in ways that open disciplinary knowledge to students' understanding and that respect students' thinking about disciplinary issues. Professors have difficulty putting themselves in the intellectual places of novices who regularly make a hash of their own elegant and hard-won formulations, for students' "misconceptions" represent everything that professors have learned to avoid on the way to becoming accomplished intellectuals. Most faculty members also would find it difficult to redesign their teaching in ways that supported much more rich and serious student learning, for their endeavor would increase the complexity of instruction, multiplying uncertainty as they enriched teaching and learning. In contrast, when teachers extend knowledge in finished form they reduce the complexity of knowledge, they constrain the uncertainties of instruction, and they limit the attentiveness required to teach. Lectures and recitations are a sort of pedagogical and emotional armor plate against the frustrations of opening classroom discourse to students' ideas, the puzzles of trying to make sense of students' ideas, the difficulties of managing disagreements among students, the frustration of students persevering on points that seem of little importance, and the discomfort and embarrassment of discussions that do not happen. When teachers decide to take much more extensive responsibility for students' learning, they open themselves to a host of associated anxieties and difficulties.

Despite easy slogans about interdependence between research and teaching, doing a much better job in the classroom would reduce the time and energy available for anything else, whether cooking dinner or doing research. Though it seems desirable to strengthen incentives for good teaching—assuming that a sensible scheme could be devised—such incentives alone would not transform teaching in colleges and universities. Like admission standards, incentives are an appealingly simple solution to a discouragingly complex problem (Cohen, 1996a).

Two Modest Proposals

Because higher education is deeply implicated in the problems of public schools, proposals to improve schools by improving higher education have considerable appeal. Though the initiatives discussed above are worthwhile, the results are likely to be modest. Higher education has many other purposes than strengthening the schools, and it has many constituents who care more about other matters than public education. That led me to ask whether there were not other steps that higher education institutions might take that would help a bit more. The proposals that follow are only roughly worked out, and would have no magically quick or large effects, but they could do additional good.

Build Knowledge About Instructional Quality

College and university educators are being pressed to make substantial improvement in instruction, but at the moment they lack the professional capacity to make two sorts of professionally and politically defensible judgments about instructional quality. Both would concern distinguishing among strong, weak, and mediocre instruction, but one use of such distinctions would be to offer assistance in improving the weak and mediocre work, whereas the other would be to make critical decisions about hiring, promotion, and tenure. The academy abounds with ideas about what should count as good teaching, and the local use of various means of self-report on instruction is widespread. But there are no common standards of instructional quality, and no signs of efforts to develop them.

It would be no mean feat to build such standards: Doing so would require a major research and development effort. Disciplinary and professional committees would have to design indicators of instructional quality, and perhaps cross-disciplinary groups would have to probe whether there could be comparable work across disciplines and professions. Academics would have to decide what sort of standards they desired, and how closely they could be tied to student achievement. They would have to cultivate debate and professional understanding at various levels of the higher education system. It probably would take at least a decade of very energetic work to develop decent draft indicators and to cultivate the beginning of professional acquaintance with them. It probably would take another five or ten years to organize field trials using draft indices, to explore their usability, to probe validity and reliability, and related matters.

Such work would be difficult and controversial, and many would find it troublesome, perhaps even an infringement on academic freedom. If it were done carefully and well, however, such work could help both to diagnose and improve teaching and learning in higher education and to create the capacity to make judgments about quality that would be defensible in decisions about hiring, promotion, and tenure, and in the legal and educational disputes that would follow. The development of such standards also would improve awareness of instructional problems and the organizational capacity to use such knowledge. Perhaps the most compelling argument for this work is that if the academy does not undertake it, outside agencies will quite likely develop and impose their own.

Disciplinary Research on Teaching and Learning

Fundamental improvement in college and university teaching seems unlikely without increased disciplinary interest in the cultivation of better knowledge about teaching and learning, and increased disciplinary capacity to produce and use such knowledge. Without disciplinary interest and capacity, university efforts to change incentives or adopt professional teaching standards are not likely to get vary far, because although the disciplines are central to universities' work, they are largely independent of universities' management.

One way to generate the needed interest and capacity in teaching and learning within disciplines would be to encourage the creation of disciplinary traditions of instructional research. The most desirable course of action would be one that produced interest in instructional research among most members in any given department, but that seems quite unlikely in an increasingly specialized academic world, in which teaching is an only intermittently high priority. The next most desirable approach would be to encourage the creation of instructional research subspecialties within disciplines. Though not optimal, it would be a radical and extraordinary change. One way to envision the result of such work is that each discipline would develop traditions of research on disciplinary teaching and learning in higher education. More concretely, one would want the likes of Sam Wineburg, Suzanne Wilson, Deborah Ball, and Magdalene Lampert doing research, writing, and teaching about disciplinary teaching and learning in disciplinary departments in institutions of higher education. At the moment we have few examples: Mathematics education is the strongest case, and it is not strong. Some math educators work in math departments, but most work in education schools. Many of those who work in math departments are curricula developers rather than students of instruction, and most concern themselves with problems of elementary and secondary rather than higher education. Alan Shoenfeld, whose research has focused on teaching and learning in higher education, is one of the few exceptions to the second unfortunate rule, but he teaches in a school of education.

One key element of such an initiative would be to invent and support programs of disciplinary research on teaching and learning, and another would be to support such work in disciplinary departments. That in turn would require a delicate balancing act—creating research traditions that drew variously on disciplinary knowledge, learning psychology, research on teaching and learning, and on the philosophical inquiries that are associated with each discipline, but creating them in ways that were rooted in disciplinary departments. Inventing these subspecialties also would require the construction of professional research communities that focused on such work, and it would require that such subspecialized work gain at least a toehold in larger disciplinary discourse and decision making. None of this would be intellectually difficult to do, and it all could be terrifically rewarding. There are, after all, deep, compelling, and significant instructional issues in each discipline that are linked to larger questions about the intellectual foundations and direction of the discipline. All such work would be organizationally and professionally difficult, however, because of disciplinary resistance to considering teaching and learning as intellectually significant. That is a sad feature of life in institutions that pay faculty to teach, but true nonetheless.

One reason I believe that this last proposal is feasible is that the issues would be compelling and central to the disciplines' intellectual agendas. Another is that work of this sort could prove itself valuable to disciplinarians and their departments for many purposes. It would help to build the foundations for professional teaching standards, were such an endeavor to be undertaken. It would help to create opportunities for disciplinary researchers to improve instruction within the disciplines, were there pressures to make such improvements. If universities ever did try to increase incentives for teaching, such research could be very useful in helping disciplinarians to respond constructively.

Both of the proposals sketched above can be justified in terms of higher education's core missions—improving knowledge and its use, and instruction. Both deal with a fundamental barrier to better instruction in higher education and the schools below, and each could help to improve things—but all of them together still would be only a few steps toward a distant goal. One reason that colleges and universities rarely offered American teachers intellectually serious education, after all, was that very few local school districts ever required teachers to have that sort of education, and many discouraged it. That condition still prevails today; though most American adults are worried about public education, most think that their local school is in good shape. If local educational authorities had required a very different sort of education, university teacher education probably would look rather different today.

Changing university and college teaching would help to change the popular demand for teaching and learning, but it is only one of many helps that would be needed, and it would take decades. It also would be a hard pull under the most benign circumstances, requiring continuing state and local political warfare, as lower school reformers now are beginning to discover in skirmishes with the Christian right and in the frequently disappointing lack of local support for higher standards. American higher education depends on demands for quality from the lower schools no less than the lower schools depend on higher education and business to demand educational quality. Those who care to promote much more rich and serious teaching and learning need to recognize that what they advocate is deeply revolutionary, and that if they succeed it will be the result of a long march through American culture and society, not a quick putsch. Many useful short-term steps can be taken, but in a democratic society, especially one whose government was so artfully designed to frustrate coherent policy, public education about public education must be a key element of change.

Notes

1. The research to which I refer arises from a study of how intellectually ambitious state instructional policies develop and are enacted by state and local educators and teachers, a study conducted in more than a dozen districts in Michigan, California, and South Carolina. The districts range from large to small and from highly urban to semirural. They include several cities—one very large and several others of medium size—and two fairly conventional suburbs. All of the districts include schools in which there are an appreciable number of disadvantaged children, and more than half are heavily attended by

such children. The research team of which I am a part has observed and interviewed in second and fifth grades, and in most cases we followed teachers' work for three to five years. I am indebted to my colleagues in that study, including Deborah Lowenberg Ball, Carol Barnes, Jennifer Borman, James Bowker, Daniel Chazan, Pamela Geist, S. G. Grant, Ruth Heaton, Nancy Jennings, Nancy Knapp, Susan Luks, Steve Mattson, Penelope Peterson, Sue Poppink, Richard Prawat, Jeremy Price, Ralph Putnam, Janine Remillard, Peggy Rittenhouse, Angela Shojgreen-Downer, James Spillane, Sarah Theule-Lubienski, Karl Wheatley, and Suzanne Wilson. The study has been supported in part by Michigan State University, and by grants to Michigan State University and the University of Michigan from the Pew Charitable Trust (Grant No. 91–04343–000), the Carnegie Corporation of New York (Grant No. B 5638), the National Science Foundation (Grant No. ESI-9153834), and the Consortium for Policy Research in Education (CPRE), which is funded by a grant from the U.S. Department of Education, Office of Educational Research and Improvement (Grant No. OERI-G-008690011). I also am indebted to the granting agencies for their assistance, but the ideas expressed here are mine, and are not necessarily shared by the grantors or my colleagues in the research.

2. For most of the history of American learning psychology few researchers seem to have noticed that learning requires forgetting. Inattention to this matter was due at least partly to the *tabula rasa* conception of mind that most English-speaking psychologists embraced. For if the mind is regarded as an empty vessel, the problem of learning is to figure out how the mind gets filled, or filled effectively, efficiently, or correctly. Only if one sees the mind as constantly trying to make sense of things might the problem of learning include how more efficient or effective sense-making supplants less-effective thought. Forgetting would be part of such supplanting. Another possible reason that American psychologists ignored forgetting was

their love affair with learning, and specifically their assumption that when it was done properly, learning was easy.

References

Bryk, A. S., Lee, V. E., and Holland, P. B. *Catholic Schools and the Common Good.* Cambridge, Mass.: Harvard University Press, 1993.

Cohen, D. K. "Rewarding Teachers for Student Performance." In S. H. Fuhrman and J. A. O'Day (eds.), *Rewards and Reform: Creating Educational Incentives That Work.* San Francisco: Jossey-Bass, 1996a.

Cohen, D. K. "Teaching: Practice and Its Predicaments." Unpublished manuscript, 1996b.

Cohen, D. K., McLaughlin, M. W., and Talbert, J. E. *Teaching for Understanding: Challenges for Policy and Practice.* San Francisco: Jossey-Bass, 1993.

Lortie, D. *Schoolteacher.* Chicago: University of Chicago Press, 1975.

Massey, W. F., Wilger, A. K., and Colbeck, C. "Overcoming 'Hollowed' Collegiality." *Change,* July/Aug. 1994, pp. 11–20.

McKeatchie, W. J., Pintrich, P. R., Lin, Y. G., and Smith, D. *Teaching and Learning in the College Classroom: A Review of the Research Literature.* Ann Arbor: National Center for Research to Improve Teaching and Learning, University of Michigan, 1986.

Powell, A., Farrar, E., and Cohen, D. *The Shopping Mall High School: Winners and Losers in the Educational Marketplace.* Boston: Houghton Mifflin, 1985.

Shulman, L. "Teaching as Community Property." *Change,* Nov./Dec. 1993, pp. 6–7.

Chapter Seven

Enhanced Academic Connections

Deweyan Waste, Ecological Pipelines, and Intellectual Vitality

Donald M. Stewart, Michael Johanek

All waste is due to isolation. Organization is nothing but getting things into connection with one another, so that they work easily, flexibly, and fully. . . . The great problem . . . on the administrative side is to secure the unity of the whole, in the place of a sequence of more or less unrelated and overlapping parts and thus to reduce the waste arising from friction, reduplication, and transitions that are not properly bridged. . . . From the standpoint of the child, the great waste in the school comes from his inability to utilize the experiences he gets outside the school in any complete and free way within the school itself; while, on the other hand, he is unable to apply in daily life what he is learning at school. [Dewey, 1899, cited in Dworkin, 1959, pp. 71, 76–78]

The primary waste with which Dewey was concerned in this 1899 lecture, in addition to "money or . . . things," was "that of human life, the life of the children while they are at school, and afterward because of inadequate and perverted preparation" (Dewey, 1899, cited in Dworkin, 1959, pp. 70–71). Countering the academic isolation that produces such intellectual waste, within and among schools and colleges, forms the focus of this chapter.

In this era of tight budgets and competing fiscal interests, our heightened concern with productivity and efficiency aptly draws our attention to the efficacy of our school-college connections. Schools and colleges connect in many ways: college graduates teach in the schools, high school students graduate and go on to college, curricular and pedagogical changes at times ripple back and forth, both levels may be affected by the same local economy or politics, and so on. In this chapter we focus almost exclusively upon the academic connections between high schools and higher education, and generally emphasize policy affecting the professionals who work in those institutions.[1] The question addressed here brings us back to Dewey: How do we so enhance the school-college academic connections so to as to prevent the wasteful intellectual isolation he described? Eventually, our answer must also address related questions, such as who will shape and control these connections, as well as which values we most wish to promote.

We contend that recent educational policy regarding school-college connections has focused "on the administrative side," and in particular, concentrated on the academic logistics of moving students from secondary to higher education. This emphasis corresponds with a primary concern for curricular alignment and accountability across the K–16 spectrum, that is, increasing the curricular connections between schools and colleges. While recognizing the need for such concerns, we suggest that schools and colleges connect in ways far more fundamental than curricular credits, admissions procedures, and assessment instruments. In their best moments, schools and colleges connect–via their teachers, professors and students–through a shared "attitude of inquiry," as Dewey put it, a shared academic enthusiasm for liberated and disciplined thought. Nurturing such intellectual excitement demands breaking the isolation of teachers and faculty in at least two ways: connecting them in conversation with each other as academic colleagues, and supporting their more robust engagement with their own intellectual undertakings. We maintain, therefore, that school-college policy should be driven and evaluated primarily by its effects on intellectual vitality, and we propose a framework in which that might be developed.

After defining these academic connections a bit further, we will present how they have been addressed in two recent policy trends, and then suggest several appropriate policy recommendations, set within a quite preliminary new framework.

Academic Connections, Potential Isolations

The academic connections between schools and colleges are myriad and complex.[2] These quite distinct institutional sectors, each with a range of institutions within the sector, do share common ground in a number of areas. Though the most obvious connections occur at the point of transition from school to college—embodied in the processes of graduation, admission, and placement—schools and colleges also "connect" in ways owing to the shared nature of their enterprise. At the risk of oversimplifying, three general goals would seem to define the majority of these school-college academic connections:

- *Alignment*: articulation of academic content and skills— that is, connecting content and expectations across levels of education

- *Accountability*: measures of quality, integrity of academic content, and effectiveness of pedagogy—that is, connecting institutions to students, families, and the public

- *Intellectual vitality*: effectiveness of the shared culture and pursuit of academic inquiry—that is, connecting educators to each other and to those in related fields, within an overall educational pursuit

Much of the attention given to questions of school-college connections by policymakers has addressed the first of these; that is, alignment, spelling out in scope and sequence the skills and knowledge to be learned at various points in a learner's academic career in given subject areas. Nearly all states and districts attempt to connect the content and expectations across various levels of schooling, and to some degree, across K–12 to higher education. Such efforts have included curriculum frameworks at the school levels, exit assessments for graduates, and efforts to align graduation requirements with first-year level study at the postsecondary level. Programs offering college-level credit to high school students, such as the Advanced Placement program and dual enrollment schemes, or explicit course requirements for university admission, illustrate two of the more concrete forms of content articulation across school-college boundaries. Publications from universities spelling out their academic expectations for incoming students provide another common example (see, for example, State University of New York, 1995). Many policymakers express the continuing need to improve the alignment of school and college programs in order to increase "learning productivity," while avoiding course content duplication and gaps by setting clear standards for the "delivery of instruction" in specific content areas and at specific grade levels.

Much attention, and not a little frustration, has also been paid to the second purpose of academic connections, which concerns those efforts to gauge the quality of teaching and learning taking place. Such accountability initiatives in effect attempt to improve the connections between students/public and the institutions that serve them. Measures have included those focusing primarily on student achievement and persistence (for example, reported test scores, graduation rates from high school and college, retention rates at university, college attendance rates, advanced placement and honors courses taken, state-mandated feedback systems) as well as, to a lesser extent, those focusing on teaching standards and teacher professional development standards.[3]

The third aim of academic connections between schools and colleges concerns the elusive characteristic of intellectual vitality. In terms of observable academic phenomena, this quality is often associated with highly interactive classroom discussions; complex problem-solving activities; creative expression through the arts; deep reflection upon texts or data; or highly analytic or synthetic reasoning, however communicated. Others have expressed the concept in terms of developed "habits of mind," though we would add perhaps what Israel Scheffler calls the "cognitive emotions" and "emotions generally in the service of critical inquiry": rational passions, perceptive feelings, theoretical imagination, the joy of verification and the feeling of surprise (Scheffler, 1991, pp. 3–17). Students in schools and colleges participate in, at some level, an intellectual pursuit, and the characteristics of such pursuits are a potential common ground shared by teachers, students, and faculty, that is, a basis for enhanced school-college connections. Schools and colleges certainly "connect" on this basis now, through the shared (to some degree) culture of academic inquiry. If in no other way, they share an intellectual culture somewhat indirectly through shared human traffic—that is, high school teachers study in colleges, and college students bring with them their academic experiences of the high school.

Overall, however, we find that the isolation of individual teachers, especially at the secondary level, but also within institutions of higher education, presents a particularly challenging obstacle to effective educational improvement because it limits the degree to which intellectual vitality can be developed and sustained. This isolation—colleagues disconnected both from each other and from their disciplines—occurs in many ways: a history professor fails to remain current with the field; a school English teacher stops reading literature; a faculty member never discusses her teaching with colleagues; or a teacher remains isolated from the broader lives of his students and the community in which he teaches. Breaking such isolation will not insure intellectual vitality, but it remains a necessary condition for its development. In the absence of intellectual vitality, a stagnant mental life can plague an institution, frustrating effective self-reflection and improvement. As Elliot Eisner has described the teaching life at the school level: "Teaching, by and large, in both elementary and secondary schools is a lonely activity. . . . Teachers see each other, but seldom in the context of teaching. . . . Despite what seems obvious, we have designed schools both physically and organizationally to restrict the teacher's access to other professionals. As a result, it is not unusual for teachers to feel that no one really cares about the quality of their work" (Eisner, 1992, pp. 613–14).[4]

Thus, while intellectual vitality may be difficult to define precisely—an area that others are far more capable of addressing—we do suggest that it can be supported by at least three types of school-college academic efforts, each working to break the isolation of individual teachers and professors:

- *Cross-level teacher-faculty programs*: Programs that facilitate a flow of ideas and innovations across institutional levels and sectors concerning content and pedagogy support greater vitality in academic inquiry. Examples of such programs would include school-college subject matter projects, teacher-faculty institutes such as at Yale–New Haven, Internet links across school and college classrooms, Advanced Placement development committees, readings and workshops, etc. (Breaking the isolation of teachers from each other within a single school seems also to contribute significantly to improvements in student achievement; see Newmann and Wehlage, 1995; Newmann, 1994; Bryk and Driscoll, 1988; Lee, Smith, and Croninger, 1995.)

- *Community linkages*: Joint school-college linkages to the local community issues and public life, especially in terms of local problem solving or addressing local concerns, provide another support to intellectual vitality. Examples include the science class in which students understand and address local ecological problems, the art class's involvement in the local art community, a public policy course involved in the resolution of a local housing crisis, or students in various disciplines involved in local schools (such as the University of Pennsylvania's WEPIC project). Promising school-to-career initiatives can build close relationships among teachers, business representatives, and postsecondary faculty, and break an isolation that often fosters outdated approaches.

- *Programmatic disjunctures*: One "linkage," if you will, that can serve intellectual vitality is the absence of too-smooth a linkage

across levels of academic work, confronting students with intellectual choices potentially productive of personal development.
Thus, for example, the process of choosing postsecondary study, or
even whether to pursue postsecondary study, can be terribly significant in the personal development of individual students in a
way that the transition from tenth to eleventh year may not be.
Well-structured and with proper guidance, the disjuncture between
schooling and higher education can result in greater intellectual
vitality resulting from those choices that force questions of personal
identity, academic interest, autonomy, etc. In turn, the teacher/
professor connects in a very vital way to the student's life, and reaf-
firms his connection to the noble purposes shared by educators
across levels.

Pursuing all three goals of school-college academic connections—alignment, accountability, and intellectual vitality—often
creates tensions and trade-offs among priorities, and recent policies
have shown a tendency to favor the first, and to some degree the
second. The third goal, in which school reform and accountability
aims appear most convergent, rarely seems to enter serious policy
discussion. How best to adjust policy so as to support all three types
of academic connections, and thus minimize Deweyan "waste," is
the challenge before us. Our responses to issues of policy control and
authority, it is suggested as well, may need to differ depending upon
the category of academic connections we wish to advance most.

A brief analysis of two recent policy trends, viewed in light of
these three goals for school-college connections, may suggest some
useful lessons as we proceed toward a revitalized policy framework.

Policy Trend Number 1:
School-College as Educational Pipeline

One strongly policy-oriented discussion concerns how school-
college academic connections might best promote higher academic
standards and greater public accountability. Among many possible

answers, one prominent approach suggests that higher education should align itself more directly with the "standards movement" and the outcomes-based education proposed for K–12. In this approach, the "standards-based" reform of K–12 should be moved "up" into higher education, primarily by setting "competency-based" admissions policies aligned to national standards. Advocates urge a seamless K–16 educational reform as the only way to sustain K–12 reform, believing that students and their parents will not take standards seriously unless colleges and universities require evidence of them in the admissions process and demand them in courses. In turn, postsecondary faculty will need to change their pedagogy, align their curriculum to emerging national standards, and assess the "value added" by their educational enterprise. (For commentary on implications for higher education, see Stewart, 1995.) Given the fierce competition for limited state funds, higher education must be able to demonstrate such "value added" if it hopes to retain substantial levels of support. Finally, unless higher education dramatically changes the way it prepares those who will end up teaching in the schools, creative K–12 curricular reforms will simply "implode," as teachers will tend to teach as they themselves were taught, leaving creative interactive pedagogies a permanently marginal practice.

In order to pursue greater alignment and accountability, many policymakers have begun to view, and ultimately therefore to attempt to manage, the compulsory and collegiate levels of education as one continuum, through which students move as they gain skills and competencies. A seamless K–16 or pipeline approach in one of its most comprehensive forms would advocate an alignment of secondary and higher education curricula, the subsequent usage of high school exit competency assessments for admission to university, and the use of college graduate exit exams in order to assess the performance of institutions of higher education.[5] "Waste," or inefficiency, results from clumsy linkages among institutions, no unifying vision, and lack of incentives for good teaching and learning.

This pipeline approach draws from some of the recent literature on "systemic" school reform, though it often does not do justice to the more thoughtful advocates of this approach (see, for example, Smith and O'Day, 1990; Fuhrman, 1993; Elmore and Fuhrman, 1994).[6] From the vantage point of state governments, pipeline policies hope to affect all schools and colleges through common curricular frameworks, linked performance assessments, and an alignment of state educational policies across the K–16 continuum. In theory, local sites would retain considerable autonomy, at least in terms of how they choose to adapt to mandated entrance and exit exams and, at the K–12 level, state-developed curricula or competencies. Pipeline advocates often draw from the "systemic" literature the need for a "coherent" centralized educational vision and a supportive state-constructed infrastructure, especially in terms of new assessments, along with an emphasis on curricular frameworks. (Given high student demand and tight education budgets, for example, remediation and course content duplication warrant immediate correction.)

As pipeline policies tend to serve primarily the goals of alignment and accountability, the goal of intellectual vitality seems less effectively supported, while less subtle accountability measures tend to take the forefront, much to the frustration of many educators. This results also from the pipeline emphasis on the immediate problem of transferring students from one institution to another—a messy process that needs to be reengineered into a more seamless series of transactions among interlocking service providers. Curricular efficiency becomes paramount; curriculum alignments and accountability assessments, the common currency of the continuum; and an orderly and efficacious skills development process, the prize.[7]

Yet, in sum, this approach represents a useful evolution of state participation in school/college improvement. On a policy level, the pipeline approach has brought welcome attention to the overall vision we have for our children's education. It shifts our focus usefully to the specifics of academic performance, and to the difficult, but essential task of defining our educational goals more clearly. A few states have taken seriously the need to develop a state-supported infrastructure more useful to improving classroom practices; the embarrassing lack of professional development time and resources for teachers may yet be addressed. The emphasis on academic competencies has encouraged promising developmental work in new assessments; state commitment to developing new assessments can spur commercial and nonprofit research and development in these areas. For all of these reasons, and as much as we will argue for the limits of this pipeline vision in addressing intellectual vitality, we must not ignore its significant contributions to other goals. To do so risks repeating education's tendency for policy patricide today as we lurch toward tomorrow's policy panacea.

On a historical note, the pipeline approach reflects a deeply held American proclivity, one which policymakers ignore at their peril. From carving out an inhabited wilderness 350 years ago to building a school system for the burgeoning urban masses at the start of this century, Americans have prized practical efficiency in education, a cool pragmatism, increasingly accompanied by the fair handmaiden of science. School-college connections emphasizing curricular content alignment and new assessment technologies often echo these themes. During the first decades of this century, many early school bureaucrats, whom historian David Tyack has called the "administrative progressives," saw the uniform curriculum, poorly trained teachers, dull recitation methods, and the undifferentiated structure as "rigid, unscientific, wasteful, and inhumane." Admiring imitators of a rising business class, they became "evangelists for new educational goals of science and social efficiency. They . . . wanted a one-best system but it was to be a more complex, differentiated organization adapted to new social and economic conditions" (Tyack, 1974, p. 188). Supportive of the pedagogical innovators who advocated the "project method" or "activity curriculum," they sought to individualize instruction, to meet the different needs of different children more humanely, and to prepare them efficiently for their likely work after school. Then as now, tough social conditions, a dramatically changing international economy and a large influx of the children of immigrants demanded that the school system adapt efficiently.

The pipeline approach tends best to develop school-college academic connections that build greater content/skill articulation (number 1), and to some degree address issues of instructional quality and content integrity (number 2). However, the academic connections that promote intellectual vitality (number 3), especially those that support the intellectual dialogue among teachers and professors, tend to be less well served for a number of reasons.

One reason may be that for many educators, there is something alienating about the pipeline emphasis on alignment and accountability, which seems to detract from its effectiveness as a basis for encouraging intellectual performance and collaboration. Ever since the "experts" prescribed "efficient" approaches like the Lancasterian system—with, contrary to much caricature, some of the best of motivations at heart—some have found the efficiency emphasis a bit debilitating.[8] They questioned what seemed an overly mechanical sense of education, a too rational and too centrally run approach, as an indication of a certain spiritual dryness and narrowness. Better to stay isolated behind closed classroom doors until this, too, passes. Was it not a caricature of life, created by our modern scientific culture, where confidence in the person had been replaced by confidence in a system, the cool delivery of a new product called curriculum, the seamless placement of human capital into the national production system? Schooling's aims seemed to shrink like a noose around the enterprise, just as access to it increased; the rhetoric followed, and classroom teachers found policy chatter a dull, lifeless description of what they thought they were about.[9]

In addition, setting academic standards for content and competencies, to the degree that the standards are seen as set remotely from particular academic communities, appears to be in tension with the intellectual vitality that such a policy means to promote. This may not be an unhealthy nor completely avoidable tension, but policy must recognize and address it. Intelligent humans can differ greatly over the intellectual ends or even means they prize, and yet each can engage in academic pursuits of equal vitality. Intellectual acuity and wisdom do not seem to increase as one moves from school site to district to state; frameworks could conceivably be generated in many different localities, without loss of quality. Indeed there is something about locally generated objectives that promise greater meaning and more enduring effectiveness, especially as common measures of academic quality are developed.

A further cultural constraint to the pipeline approach, indeed even to its goal of administrative efficiency, is the fact that the school-college transition functions as a coming-of-age ritual for many American adolescents. The school-college transition cannot be isolated from its wider cultural significance. If properly tapped, such a personal passage can be a wellspring of intellectual growth, a decision to develop academically and personally in a given direction based on a broad inspection of one's life goals. This echoes a deep chord in American culture, for the school-college transition is emblematic of this society's persistent and periodic efforts at cultural revival, social reconstruction, and civic reawakening (McLoughlin, 1978). Higher education does not represent simply an extension of high school content to more difficult competency levels, a movement simply in subject matter scope and sequence; high school is not justified simply as a preparation for postsecondary education. Whether efficient or not, certain disjunctures across these sectors may in fact promote greater intellectual vitality, particularly at the postsecondary level, as young adults are forced to make explicit certain fundamental decisions about their lives.

The school and academy represent quite different sets of purposes and carry out different roles within this republic. As a consequence—one with educational implications—the personal transition across these sectors carries with it the cultural emphasis on self-development and maturation as growing autonomy. From a heavily mandated curriculum, one elects to associate with a given academic community based on shared interests, on qualities of mind sought and trained. In moving from compulsory to voluntary schooling, one shifts from democracy's workshop to its more fluid intellectual plaza. From the still local high school to the more cosmopolitan university, one glimpses firsthand the rich cultural and intellectual diversity of this land. Though we may not always tap its potential, the school-college transition nevertheless reflects the profound desire of a transplanted people to cultivate themselves in a land of shallow roots. The transition embodies both personal and public renewal. Whether a Russian Jew at New York's City College early this century or a Dominican immigrant at Miami-Dade Community College today, Americans still believe in a future that is, at least partially, self-constructed; the school-college connection must be so structured as to tap the intellectual vitality of this culturally laden disjuncture. For it is within this transition process and its imposed rites of self-definition and self-renewal that we determine our own educational ends, collectively shaping what Lawrence Cremin called "the American paideia" (Cremin, 1988, p. ix). As much as Americans prize the social efficiency noted above, they—including the teachers and professors—also seem to value deeply this academic disjuncture as reflective of a rite of personal development in a highly individualistic culture.

Policy Trend Number 2: Enhancing the Immediate School-College Transition

A second policy trend over the last decade, not entirely separated from the first, attempts in some ways to answer this trade-off between respecting different institutional missions and the logistical needs for efficient student transitions. As such, it must be recognized as another quite promising development in education for quite different reasons than the evolving pipeline policies. This second trend echoes the innovative efforts of what historian Tyack refers to as the "pedagogical progressives" throughout this century (Tyack, 1974).

Some school reformers—enthused by the promise of more interactive pedagogies, performance assessments, student portfolios, and greater school site autonomy—express the fear that current admissions processes will frustrate their reform efforts. School reform has been developing numerous models of K–12 schooling, whereas higher education often seems unaware and unaccommodating. Admissions offices, claim these reformers, too often mechanically calculate a student's educational opportunity based on credit total, course titles, seat time, test scores, class rank, and GPAs. Thus, some school reformers want admissions officers to recognize and deal with the alternative curricula, at times distinctive to their school community, that they have developed in an effort to be creatively responsive to student needs. They want colleges to handle more comprehensive pictures of students than numbers can suggest, and accommodate the innovative and diverse experimentation characteristic of many alternative and progressive schools. If colleges fail to accommodate the schools, legitimate parental anxieties will put the lid on percolating reforms. Experiment all you wish, just do not disadvantage my child's chance of admission to State U!

Here is a dilemma well worth debating: how can institutional articulation be made to accommodate the distinct missions of varied institutions in disparate contexts, encouraging richly diverse and intellectually rigorous academic communities rather than fostering a bland gray homogeneity across schools? The challenge involves real interests, veritable dilemmas, and honest differences. Member associations like the College Board have been involved in this for nearly a century; the SAT itself, designed not to dictate secondary school curriculum, originated in part as a means of accommodating the diverse secondary curricula that arose during the Progressive era in public schooling (Valentine, 1987).

Here is also a conversation that can be productively resolved in diverse ways.[10] Several emerging technologies should help support the articulation between increasingly varied schools and equally diverse colleges. For example, various electronic college application networks and World Wide Web sites, both of postsecondary institutions and educational services groups, offer those students who have access extensive information regarding possible postsecondary options, funding sources, and application logistics. Other innovations include computer adaptive testing, for both admissions and placement purposes; "dynamic assessments," instruments that assess student ability to learn through a task; instruments able to evaluate a student's ability to generate alternative explanations; the digitized portfolio; open-ended tasks and simulations; and instruments linking student performance to specific guidance resources.

Several university system efforts to accommodate diverse school improvement efforts are also under way in Wisconsin, Colorado, Oregon, and California. Wisconsin's effort, which builds in a research component comparing traditional and nontraditional admissions protocols, offers an example of the kind of measured accommodation universities are beginning to develop. The Transition Project in California, Oregon's PASS Project, and a growing collaboration between the College Board and the Coalition of Essential Schools represent just a few of the many state, regional, and national efforts to adjust college admissions procedures to alternative school models.[11] The efforts have only recently begun, and few generalizations can be made yet. However, each promises to lend additional experience and data to the emergence of a more accommodating articulation infrastructure.

We have, then, the potential in the emerging technologies and collaborations to build a variegated articulation infrastructure able to handle the increasing diversity of educational institutions and students. This may allow us—and here is its great promise—to minimize the trade-offs between school-college policies that enhance articulation and accountability with those that support greater intellectual vitality. But to do so may require a policy framework better able to encourage intellectually rigorous, intrinsically humane, and locally adaptive institutions.

Advancing All Three Goals—Some Initial Premises

Building from the two recent policy trends just described, upon what premises might policymakers construct a renewed framework for school-college policies in order to advance all three goals— alignment, accountability, and intellectual vitality? We postulate the following minimum premises for such a framework:

Encourage Teaching/Learning Qualities Directly, Let Institutional Articulation Follow

Whereas policy must address institutional linkages per se in such matters as credit policies and admissions requirements, policymakers must directly seek to assess and encourage the teaching/learning qualities they value. Teachers and faculty must be engaged directly in this process as agents of change, or we risk developing more policies that never penetrate the "black box" of the classroom. Getting beyond the classroom door means engaging those who determine most what happens there, teachers and students. Institutional articulation may support such changes but are terribly indirect in affecting the changes.

In addition, an institutional policy focus weakens policy to the degree that educational institutions are evolving ever more rapidly. A "seamless vision" approach will forever be frustrated as both sides of the seam continue to diversify, multiply, and transform themselves in response to their environments and constituencies—even if they continue to carry the familiar labels of school or college. Educators from K–12 through higher education face a series of trends that may reconfigure dramatically the array and nature of institutions we use to educate ourselves; this reconfiguration has been more the norm than the exception in U.S. history (Cremin, 1976, 1988). More ethnically diverse, linguistically challenged, economically disadvantaged, and vocationally oriented students enter our schools and universities each year; nearly 50 percent of postsecondary students are over 25 years of age (Aslanian, 1996).

Virtual higher education expands as national frontiers dissolve.[12] Commercial firms have gone beyond supplying services to schools and colleges; increasingly they are themselves delivering educational services. One for-profit university in the Southwest has tripled its enrollments in five years, and claims to be the nation's twelfth-largest accredited private university (Stecklow, 1994). High-tech megamergers promise highly capitalized contenders; corporations already spend perhaps $200 billion on education every year (Eurich, 1990, p. 18). With an increasingly diverse student body, evolving and emerging educational institutions, multiple and varied educational transitions, and the unpredictable role of technological innovation in changing the educational experiences, policies guided by a K–16, curriculum-specific and institutionally bound framework will probably be ineffective in affecting the teaching/learning dynamic.

Curriculum and Assessment Are Useful as Tools, Less So as Reliable Levers

Policymakers must recognize that institutional culture, taught curricula and assessment practices are the variables we need to affect, not fixed tools for improving schools and colleges. High standards can exist in an endless variety of curricula. To stimulate better curricular quality, stimulate greater professional and organizational capacity, and begin by breaking the intellectual isolations separating teachers and faculty (Darling-Hammond, 1993; O'Day, Goertz, and Floden, 1995). Using new assessments to drive curriculum and instructional reform, on the other hand, can be quite problematic. The contribution of an assessment's format to a teacher's pedagogy has perhaps been seriously overstated (Noble and Smith, 1994a, 1994b; Shepard and others, 1995). In addition, if we are to avoid educational hubris, we must recognize that many of our finest educational ambitions for our students may always involve, as Eliott Eisner puts it, "forms of performance for which the pre-definition of outcomes cannot be specified" (Eisner, 1994,

p. 14). Not surprisingly, the drive to establish a "coherent" curriculum or a single set of standards across institutions arises far more
from policy and political circles than from teachers and professors.

Finally, too much reform depends on assessments that do not
yet exist in reliable or affordable forms. This runs the risk of frustrating the best of school reform by the imposition of poorly-
designed, but fiscally-feasible instruments, a tendency already
evident. The clear technical constraints, not to mention those
more political in nature, are one reason states are refusing to rush
into new assessments.[13]

Different Levels of Authority May Advance Different Goals

Though state-level authority may serve alignment and, to some
extent, accountability goals, the traditions of local control and
institutional autonomy, however they may have shifted over the
years, remain strong and vibrant forces affecting policy impact on
intellectual vitality. Recent controversies over mandated curricula
should reinforce this point to any would-be reformer. Change
within educational institutions—in schools, for example, as seen
in the efforts of the Coalition of Essential Schools, Levin's efforts,
Comer's initiatives, TQM-inspired changes, SBM/SDM designs,
effective schools—depends in no small part upon each institution
setting the outcomes and mission it deems important. Further, as
Judith Warren Little has argued, "One test of teachers' professional
development is its capacity to equip teachers individually and collectively to act as shapers, promoters, and well-informed critics of
reforms" (Little, 1994, p. 106).

Obviously each school need not reinvent the wheel or isolate
itself from other schools' curricula; student mobility is also a serious
concern. Setting local standards demands reference to nonlocal
standards for comparison. However, school change literature makes
clear that externally determined and mandated content and performance standards do not tend to nurture school reform that is
likely to affect classroom practice (Cuban, 1993; Cohen and

Spillane, 1992). At the postsecondary level, it is clear, if only from the recent reactions to mandated efforts, that imposed assessments and curricula will only meet with deeply resentful opposition (Peters, 1994). Many professors would view this as a crude application of school reform methods to the very different world of the academy. In the end, mandates do little to remedy the academic isolations that so debilitate intellectual vitality.

Instead of avoiding controversy by stating only vague curricular goals over a broad range of institutions, we should stimulate a rich variety of purposes and missions, within the shared bounds of a democratic people, and then provide the tools by which students, families, and the public can gauge their success or failure according to the mission the institution set out for itself.

We Need More Tools!

Perhaps we will know that we are serious about school reform when attention increases to developing and testing the tools by which teachers, counselors, admissions officers, and professors will actually transform school-college connections. In commercially viable areas such as electronic application networks or some administrative supports, a number of for-profit and nonprofit ventures are actively involved. In the vast majority of areas in which educators need better curricular and assessment support tools, research and development is scarce.

For example, if admissions procedures are to accommodate a greater variety of high school academic programs, such as those not based on Carnegie units or class time, then counselors and admissions officers will need credible instruments establishing "academic currencies" by which to evaluate student abilities, handle different and possibly a much broader range of student data, place accepted nontraditional applicants effectively, and justify nonadmission decisions to anxious families. In other words, we would need to develop and maintain a robust variety of credible academic "currencies" as standards rather than standardizing curriculum into an interinstitutional "currency." The fact remains that too few such R&D efforts are underway and fewer are likely to be sustained.

Another category of examples concerns the academic interventions, diagnostic instruments, relational databases or pedagogical tools that will support the achievement of new academic standards in the average classroom. Notwithstanding the considerable professional development that may be necessary, even trained teachers and faculty will require practical, well-tested tools to support these efforts—whether they be in the form of powerful new software programs, classroom strategies targeted toward higher-order thinking skills, or diagnostic instruments linked to pedagogical and counseling resources. These tools, if a product of continuing professional consensus, also serve practically to connect teachers and professors with best practice in the field.

In addition, equity demands that new assessment instruments continue to reflect both specific curricula and those skills developed in a variety of strong curricula, and this requires continued investment. Making college admission solely dependent upon a uniform curriculum or set of subject-specific competencies, while serving alignment goals, will frustrate educational equity. Students from those schools lacking such a curriculum, no matter how competent or self-schooled, will be shut out of educational opportunities.[14] Thus, while subject matter assessments certainly must play an important role, exclusive reliance on them in a seamless curricula-aligned system could have a tremendously adverse impact on the most underserved populations, and limit the ability of this society to develop neglected talents. As testing expert Robert Linn stated concerning the SAT (I), "[It] provides a second chance. . . . For many students, [it] provides an alternate way of demonstrating scholastic ability that may not be reflected in high school grades or in performance on subject-matter achievement tests" (Linn, 1994, p. 30). For this reason, a variety of instruments not directly dependent upon specific curricula continue to require ongoing research and development.

The Ecology of School-College Connections

Based on these premises, we need to construct another framework for school-college policies. Rather than indirectly trying to influence teaching/learning by changing the format of assessments or by changing the curriculum guidelines—both of which may effectively serve alignment and accountability—we propose asking what we want to happen inside the classroom, and what kind of educational ecology is needed to support it.[15] This organic/ecological framework would start from the qualities of interaction that constitute effective learning experiences, seeking to stimulate rich teaching/learning dynamics across institutions, linked by the principles and practices that underlie such processes.[16] Primary linkages across academic levels would be based in research-informed principles of the teaching/learning process, and upon shared public pursuit of richer educational ecologies. Curricular alignment across large heterogeneous sectors would become an occasionally useful byproduct rather than a central focus of policy, with student transitions only one of many ways in which schools and colleges connect. Success would not be measured primarily by the "seamlessness" of student transitions, but rather by the quality of the learning stimulated across institutions, the intellectual vitality prodded by various school-college connections.

From a pipeline image, policy primarily links schools to colleges by aligning curricula and assessments. From an ecological image, policy primarily should help students and teachers gauge and stimulate high-quality educational interactions by building a shared language of research-informed principles and best practices, and by meeting needs for institutional articulation through tools tested to reflect these shared principles.

Thus, in addition to constructing a better pipeline across institutions, we also start from inside the classroom and link institutions via the common "biology" of teaching/learning. What is it about the process of teaching and learning that we desire? What is the

Figure 7.1. Educational Ecology: Three Spheres of Interaction

Sphere of Immediate Practice	the teaching/learning dynamic in which the learner is directly involved
Institutional Sphere	the interaction between sphere one's dynamic and the institutional environment in which it occurs (school organization and culture)
External Sphere/Context	the interaction between that institution and the wider context of constituencies, community, policies, and personnel preparation

environment, the ecology (in the classroom, in the school, and in the system/community) needed for that process to flourish? Although we would have a healthy respect for natural processes we do not completely understand, we would also need some practical tools for a learning community to distinguish between weeds and roses.

How might we picture such an ecology of school-college connections? For simplicity, we have identified three interlocking concentric spheres that affect a student's experience. The educational ecology's core interaction concerns the complex process of teaching/learning itself, which in turn is influenced by its immediate and extended environment. For this discussion, the spheres are described in Figure 7.1 and are contrasted in Figure 7.2 with a pipeline approach.

The qualities of interaction within and across spheres at schools and colleges—for example, the incidence of student analysis in math classrooms, or the degree of a university's engagement in community problem solving—would form the core focus of educational research, and the resulting research-informed principles would provide the common ground of discussion, the basis for qualitative, educational linkages across institutions and sectors. Evaluations and assessments based on these principles would provide the

Figure 7.2. Pipeline View Versus Ecological View of School-College Connections

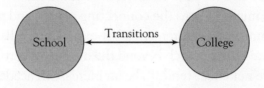

A Pipeline View of School-College Connections

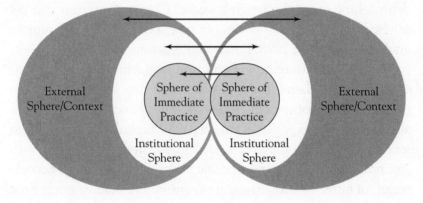

An Organic/Ecological View of School-College Connections

basis for credible "currencies"—a shared language of quality for educators and the public—by which largely autonomous institutions with varied missions can be better described and understood within the "marketplace" of educational opportunities. Some exist today, providing level-headed and hard-nosed accountability without stultifying pipeline prescriptions, both as "curriculum-neutral" (in one narrow function, the SAT serves this purpose) assessments and as curricula of recognized quality (for example, Advanced Placement or International Baccalaureate). Much more needs to be done.

Examples of Ecology-Minded School-College Policy

In order to clarify what this means to policy, let us consider the goal of more rigorous academic challenges for students. With a pipeline in mind we might look to the connecting points, and raise graduation and admission requirements. Yet experience tells us that it is difficult to raise them much beyond the median of current practice, and that the net effect tends to be an increase in academic course-taking among lower-achieving students (see note 15). Combined with increased admission requirements at local universities and proper guidance support, the impact increases, with even more students taking more challenging work.[17] Course content might get watered down, but most classroom practices probably will remain unchanged (Porter, 1995; Porter and Associates, 1994).

A more ambitious pipeline notion might inspire a rethinking of requirements themselves, away from seat-time in courses to competencies or performances, as several states have attempted or are attempting. The experience has been educational in itself, and a bit sobering. Competencies too vague become shelf-sitters along with past packets of policy prose. Specific performance standards become targets of bitter controversy, and expensive assessments rarely exist at a defensible stage of development. Issues of whose standards are being imposed inevitably flare. Admissions personnel, although often sympathetic to the reform aims, must themselves seek reliable standards of comparability and efficient placement instruments. Under fiscal constraints, controversy-averse politicians shy away from dramatic curricular or assessment reforms, though some may still propose radical shifts in governance. Those teachers and faculty involved in developing new performance standards often benefit considerably from the professional development opportunity it represents, though they may also represent largely the converted. As the initiatives ebb, so do such opportunities, and most teachers watch the froth of reform disappear onto the vast beach of unaffected classroom practice.

If, on the other hand, we accept the ecology framework, how would we design policy? First, we would set as our primary goal enhancing the intellectual vitality in school and college class-rooms. Second, we would build ongoing school-college collaborations, starting with teachers and faculty, through which to break down intellectual isolations and to construct educationally sound means for gauging the qualities of academic inquiry. Third, after bringing in public and student constituencies, we would refine and disseminate publicly these gauges of intellectual vitality. The public education campaign this would involve would bring accountability pressures to bear as close to the classroom as possible and focus upon the quality of the academic enterprise.

To oversimplify, we would need to address two sets of factors: those that build academic connections that in turn build capacity for more engaging teaching practices (to professionalize standards-building) and those that bring accountability pressures more directly to bear on what happens in classrooms (to "localize" incentives for improvement).

Breaking Academic Isolations, Gauging Intellectual Vitality

First, we must invest in teachers and faculty. In order to increase an institution's capacity for improving classroom practices, teachers need joint planning time (at least at K–12 and some initial post-secondary levels), responsive professional development opportunities, and collaborative networks of peer faculty and institutions. Professional standard-building networks promote both improvement and accountability while breaking the deadly isolation of too many who teach in closed rooms. These needs are well known and documented.

In addition, however, teachers and professors need cooperatively to develop "currencies" of academic standards— gauges of academic quality, curriculum- and noncurriculum-specific, that are credible to diverse institutions—including minimum standards of pedagogy.[18] Such standards must be openly and broadly developed and subject to consistent review. They may be multiple, reflecting distinctive categories of educational mission. They must also be enforced by colleagues through mechanisms such as accreditation review teams and peer classroom observations. We realize that this causes shudders in many of our colleagues. We recognize further that some of our best teachers seem most distant from the realms of teacher associations and professional jargon.

Yet however idiosyncratic successful teaching and classrooms can be, we all implicitly recognize practices that should not be allowed, and could probably agree upon 70 to 80 percent of the attributes of a classroom with effective student engagement. As educators we must find a way to say this to each other, and to represent this to the public so that they will be better equipped to reject poor practices. Current experimentation with classroom applications of cognitive psychology's recent insights suggest sources for possible higher-end standards of practice as well. Efforts such as the QUASAR initiative, David Perkins's and Howard Gardner's various projects (Project Zero, for example), and work done under the McDonnell Foundation's Cognitive Studies for Educational Practice (CSEP) offer exciting school-college collaborations centered upon each sector's contribution to advancing research-informed principles of practice (Bruer, 1993a, 1993b; Gardner, 1981; Gardner and Boix-Mansilla, 1994; Perkins, 1992; Druckman and Bjork, 1994). The existence of "classroom" standards will greatly assist educators in peer-review processes, as well as in representing improvements in teaching to a skeptical public.[19]

Breaking Academic Isolations: Recommendation

Here we offer a specific example of an "ecological" policy approach to breaking academic isolations, one that also begins to build consensual norms of practice for intellectually vital classrooms, using accreditation/quality review teams.

Rather than move mandated monitoring from secondary schools to the academy, policymakers should consider ways of bringing a revitalized and publicly credible accreditation/peer review process to K–12. Given the increased and desired variety of K–12 institutions, and the recognized need for greater site autonomy, such an approach may represent a natural evolution in accountability design. A comprehensive system, with visiting teams composed of K–12, higher education, and community leaders, would also promote both formal and informal academic connections among faculty and teachers, while providing a valuable professional development opportunity.[20]

Higher education might in turn learn valuable lessons, given K–12's greater public exposure. For example, higher education must develop better means for appropriate public disclosure of visiting team reports, as one way of building an external sphere that more effectively stimulates good practices. K–12/postsecondary quality review teams might provide useful experiences for the regional accreditation bodies.

Students, families, and the tax-paying public have a legitimate right to demand quality. Yet, academic freedom, institutional autonomy, and bonafide expertise legitimately restrict the degree to which that right should impinge on faculty decisions about what and how they teach. A balance must be sought. Standards of professional practice must be developed to buttress an ecological approach that insures academic freedom and institutional diversity; if not, approaches focused almost solely upon alignment and accountability will continue to attract support.

Real Accountability for Intellectual Vitality

As teachers and faculty are provided with resources for professional development and collaboration, accountability must move from indirect measures of the teaching/learning process via tests of achievement on remotely determined curricula to more immediate pressures for teachers and students to pursue rigorous intellectual activities. In other words, a teacher's environment must encourage, or even prod, what by professional consensus are good teaching practices. Given the political context and culture of American schooling, the most effective route may be to educate parents and other citizens—in terms of specific, research-informed "currencies"— about the qualities that should apply to teaching and learning in their schools and colleges. In shifting from pipeline to ecology, accountability shifts from common curriculum and assessments to common currencies of academic quality and well-informed participants across the school-college continuum. A better-informed community can serve as a powerful impetus to improvement, one likely actually to affect practices, but a concerted educational effort must be made to do this.[21] More nuanced institutional profiles or school report cards may provide one important tool; "educational impact statements" from policymakers regarding their decisions would be another.[22] This is where public schooling's effectiveness depends upon successful education of the public.

Here is a terribly useful if less glamorous role for state education agencies. Might not federal or state agencies, in collaboration with professional associations, consider experimenting with creative, direct, and sustained informational efforts aimed at parents and the public? Actual tasks that students at different levels should be able to perform, teacher practices shown to be ineffective, and parental activities linked to student success might be included. Might such an effort, sustained over several years, not be more likely than one-shot exams to create consistent pressures close enough to actual classrooms to nudge appropriate changes? Or might they at least spark the kind of local conversations that might clarify institutional purposes?

Accountability for Intellectual Vitality: Recommendations

To encourage "localized" accountability pressures, we suggest the following:

• *Educational truth-in-labeling.* If institutions are to defend (and at K–12, increase) their autonomy and academic freedom, and if distant political authority is not to thwart sustained intellectual vitality, then educators must bring about a consensus-driven mechanism for proper disclosure of institutional information, one that meets the common interests of all stakeholders.

Students need far better information regarding any educational institution they are about to enter. Requiring—yes, requiring—educational institutions at all levels to present prospective students and their families a standard list of characteristics or indices, in a common format, to be determined largely within the education community, could go a long way in furthering the education of students regarding the institutions they attend. Such an educationally sensitive market-linked arrangement would contribute toward a more dynamic and locally sensitive accountability scheme. Emerging experiences with school report cards and, perhaps to a significantly lesser extent, higher education feedback systems, might offer some guidelines.

In addition, we recommend regular public information or public education campaigns concerning educational innovations and measures. Schools and colleges need to cooperate in a broader public education effort regarding their successes and challenges. Not only do we lack basic data in education, we often lack a public informed—and less often enthused—about current innovations and directions.[23] Some research suggests that fairly dramatic changes, such as to assessment instruments, may be better received if the public gains greater familiarity (Shepard and Bleim, 1995). Even a wider and more public-friendly dissemination of basic findings regarding the effects of contextual factors on student achievement (for example, from the National Assessment of Educational Progress discussing studies at home, amount of TV watching) could perform a terribly useful public service.

- *Assessment of accountability for public ends.* We cannot avoid assessing educational institutions at all levels, though particularly at compulsory stages, in terms of the public goals we set for them; that is, the academic connections schools and colleges should both make to the public good. Here the external sphere of the democratic community must be addressed. Does School/College X further the democratic development of its community, or is its faculty isolated from the intellectual challenges current problems pose? We may need to restate explicitly the public aims of schools and colleges.

We suggest schools and colleges can be made accountable, in a way consistent with increasing intellectual vitality, through local problem solving. Schools and colleges should join with other local educational agencies in the resolution of local concerns. The University of Pennsylvania leads an interesting movement in this direction with university-assisted community schooling. Higher and secondary education must seize a leadership role in the resolution of the social problems plaguing our society. Otherwise, lacking community within and vibrant relations to the wider community, the promise of campus-based improvement, indeed institutional autonomy itself, may be threatened; the wider ecology will simply not sustain a lifeform isolated in its midst.

An organic model thus attempts to exploit the vitality of local autonomy and academic freedom, allowing creative excellence and reflective practice to gain priority over efficiency and control. Our goal is not to create a systemic change per se—we have no one "system" in mind—but to stimulate the capacity to improve intellectual vitality, to gauge its quality, and to help its participants insist upon professional integrity. The intellect needs friends, and policy should be one.

Conclusion

We have no wish simply to change policy rhetoric. We must instead evolve to a richer school-college policy premise, one more aligned with heterogeneity, local control, and institutional autonomy. The ecology framework suggests a more nuanced and measured approach to improving what actually happens in classrooms, anchored in what we know and need to know about teaching and learning, and structured to break the wasteful isolations within and among our educational institutions.

Much of the experience in current academic improvement efforts suggests that we reorient policy explicitly toward teachers, faculty, and intellectual vitality. Both common sense and recent research indicate that the variables "most important to learning outcomes were those that were directly tied to students' engagement with the material to be learned" (Wang, Haertel, and Walberg, 1990, p. 37; Wang, Haertel, and Walberg, 1995). Much of "systemic" or pipeline style reforms fail to focus on such nonstructural elements critical to the student's intellectual engagement, such as teacher knowledge, classroom roles, "teachers' opportunities to learn," "external normative structures for practice," or teacher/faculty incentives (Cohen and Spillane, 1992; Elmore, 1996). The history of school reform suggests that we need a much greater effort to "enlist and honor teachers as the key people in reforming schooling" (Tyack, 1995, p. 211). Research based on an ecological model should facilitate such changes as it gauges policies' effects upon the central teaching/learning dynamic in measurable ways and seeks to enhance those school-college connections most productive of intellectual vitality.

Much more research and development are needed; we have barely begun what we need to do as a profession if intellectual vitality is ever to be taken as seriously as alignment and accountability as an explicit policy goal for schools and colleges.[24] We must admit the degree to which we do not know what effects policy actions have on classroom practices. Our lack of data, particularly longitudinal, concerning the kinds of interactions taking place in classrooms is disheartening; we cannot claim to make them our top priority if we are not willing to rectify that gap. Few other professions or industries would operate under such a lack of basic information and development work. Here is a legitimate role for government support, assisting educators in their efforts to gauge systemic changes without imposing a system externally.

Once we decide to support the core interaction of teaching, we are forced to ask difficult questions about which intelligent citizens can disagree: for example, what qualities we want for that interaction, what outcomes we want in terms of the institution's core practices, what means will best gauge our progress and shortcomings, and which "we" will be empowered to answer these concerns. That may be a far more difficult set of questions to answer than which biology text should be bought or which admissions process be implemented.

A shift to an ecological framework also forces us to address questions of purpose and mission, questions research alone cannot decide for us. Schools and colleges do not exist simply as transmitters of curriculum decided elsewhere; they are living communities of humans who must decide what matters for children, and how to implement those decisions. They need better tools and support in order to be able to do so in an effective and accountable way. In all such vital areas, governments should support changes determined by institutions and communities rather than direct changes they will limply follow or creatively subvert. As much as policymakers and even educators express frustration at often laborious and contentious local decision making, getting around school boards, teachers, and faculty accomplishes little save alienation. Providing the tools and resources for better local decision making and accountability, coupled with support for the professional infrastructure required, comprises government's most useful contribution. Accountability and alignment can then become allies of academic improvement and intellectual vitality.

Schools and colleges link most fundamentally not at their exit and entrance points, but in their shared core pursuit of ideas and queries, in enlarging hearts and minds. For in the end, schools and colleges are neither joints in a pipeline nor verdant ecologies; they are the people who inhabit them. We suggest that how we envision their shared pursuit of intellectual vitality matters, and can help shape policies that either inhibit or nurture the success of their core enterprise. If we view and talk about these academic connections in ways truer to their daily complexities, we may actually break a few stifling isolations, and transition young minds across new intellectual portals.

It is . . . as true in the school as in the university that the spirit of inquiry can be got only through and with the attitude of inquiry. The pupil must learn what has meaning, what enlarges his horizon, instead of mere trivialities. He must become acquainted with truths, instead of things that were regarded as such fifty years ago, or that are taken as interesting by the misunderstanding of a partially educated teacher. It is difficult to see how these ends can be reached except as the most advanced part of the educational system is in complete interaction with the most rudimentary. [Dewey, 1899, cited in Dworkin, 1959, p. 80]

Notes

1. For a recent survey of school-college collaborations, see Carriuolo (1995); this essay builds in part from Stewart (1995), a chapter in that survey.
2. We will use "college" simply as shorthand to mean any postsecondary institution. We also wish to recognize at the outset that academic connections represent a subset of the various educational connections linking schools and colleges, and an even smaller subset of the educational connections affecting individual student lives.
3. Some examples of measures focusing on teaching standards and teacher professional development standards include peer teacher review projects; evaluation of explicit teacher performance criteria; continuing teacher education requirements and mandatory teacher testing; work of the National Board for Professional Teaching Standards; the PRAXIS series of the Educational Testing Service; postsecondary evaluation efforts, such as those tracked and developed by the National Center on Postsecondary Teaching, Learning and Assessment.
4. That teacher isolation is a recurring obstacle can be seen in Ella Flagg Young's 1901 dissertation, "Isolation in the Schools." Young, a veteran of the Chicago school system, was a strong teacher advocate and an important collaborator with John Dewey (see Lagemann, 1996).
5. We do not pretend to capture the wide variety of meanings often ascribed to *seamless reform* as it appears in the literature,

and limit our discussion to the prominent but ultimately flawed notion we identify here. In fact, we argue that the pipeline approach fails to capture much of the richness of the literature on "systemic" reform, as well as other descriptions of comprehensive school/college reform efforts. For a sense of the variety of meanings and origins to *seamless* notions, see, for example, Dolan (1994), Fitzsimmons and Peters (1994), Mitchell (1992), Lara and Mitchell (1986), Wiggins (1991), Haycock (1994), Speaker's Blue Ribbon Commission on Career/Technical Education (1992), Gagnon (1993).

6. One of the most recent definitions of "systemic reform" is an approach to policy that seeks "meaningful reforms in schools" through "state initiatives that set clear and ambitious learning goals and standards, align all of the available policy levers in support of reform, stimulate school-level initiatives, and mobilize human and fiscal resources to support these changes" ("Reforming Science, Mathematics, and Technology Education," 1995, p. 3).

7. This pipeline view, still popular among many policymakers, also accompanies a tendency, not new to our era, to speak the language of economic rationalism in education. Education is viewed increasingly as a private consumer good, one more service in a service-saturated society. The ultimate success of the pipeline vision is an unimpeded flow of human capital along a seamless continuum of interchangeable educational delivery systems. For an interesting vision of an "unbundled" higher education as a set of service providers, see Armajani, Heydinger, and Hutchinson (1994).

8. On the Lancasterian system, see Reigart (1969), Kaestle (1973). It is interesting to note, and we should not overlook, the strong argument for Lancaster's approach on the grounds of increasing educational opportunity. Pipeline approaches, to the degree that they draw on such systemic reform literature that we have cited, also arise from strong concerns for equitable educational opportunity.

9. As the school board president of Middletown wryly put it in the 1920s: "For a long time all boys were trained to be President. Then for a while we trained them all to be professional men. Now we are training boys to get jobs" (Lynd and Lynd, 1929, cited in Lazerson, 1987, p. 198). Or as Brown University President Vartan Gregorian more recently asked, "Have we simply come to value education for what it will give us and not what it will make of us?" (quoted in Moyers, 1989, p. 185).

10. For an account of a recent colloquium addressing the implications of K–12 school reform for the admissions process cosponsored by American College Testing and the College Board, for members of the Association of Chief Admissions Officers of Public Universities, see American College Testing and College Entrance Examination Board (1994).

11. Further information on The Transitions Project is available from Pacific Educational Group, 542 Emerson Street, Palo Alto, CA 94301; on PASS, see "Frequently Asked Questions" and "Admissions Standards: Content and Process Areas Proficiencies and Indicators," both available from the Oregon State System of Higher Education, Office of Academic Affairs, P.O. Box 3175, Eugene, OR 97403–0175; for information on the College Board/CES collaboration, contact Robert Solomon or Mike Johanek at The College Board, 45 Columbus Ave., New York, NY 10023.

12. Two examples:
Open University, see http://cszx.open.ac.uk/zx/; Western Virtual University, see http://www.westgov.org/smart/vu/vu.html.

13. Vermont's experience has only been one example of the promising, but as yet still quite limited, state of enriched assessments. Few states have worked to sustain such local-level support through the inevitable challenges of so ambitious a reform effort. See, among others, Koretz, Stecher, Klein, and McCaffrey (1994); Koretz and others (1994); Klein (1994); Koretz, Stecher, and Debert (1992); Bond, Friedman, and van der Ploog (1994); Bond and Roeber (1995); Lawrence (1996).

14. This is not to be confused with simply raising requirements, whether at the high school or college admissions level, which can have substantial effects, if by nature primarily at lower competency levels. The preferred approach would appear to be a combination of coordinated increases, supported by professional development for faculty involved in teaching to new standards. See Clune (1989); Clune and White (1992); Massell, Fuhrman, and Associates (1994); Clune and others (1991).

15. We have chosen *ecology* and *organic* to recognize the need to treat the teaching/learning act as one intimately woven into and shaped by the environment in which it operates. We are aware also of two historical roots, namely the discussions in urban sociology (especially via the University of Chicago's Park and Burgess, but also New York University's early educational sociology), and discussions among settlement houses early in this century.

16. In contrast, the pipeline vision, pivoting along an institutional axis, seeks to better coordinate and control linkages across conceptually static institutions via presumed outcomes. For all of their apparent allure of accountability, pipeline policies ultimately fail to hold schools accountable for the quality of their core enterprise, that is, the teaching/learning process. Outcomes assessments are an essential but terribly indirect and inefficient way to make schools accountable for the central process to which they are dedicated.

17. "Report on the College Preparatory Initiative,"presented to the Board of Trustees, City University of New York; my thanks to vice chancellor Elsa Nunez-Wormack and her staff for their assistance. See also Newman (1995).

18. Though we do not share the misguided faith that leads some to try to make a natural science of teaching, we do recognize that guidelines informed by research and experience can help institutions to target their improvement efforts and to evaluate policies in truly educational terms. As simply one example, see

Presidential Task Force on Psychology in Education, American
Psychological Association (1993).
19. Similar standards need to be developed for institutional and
external spheres as well, based on how practices there affect
teaching/learning. Decisions regarding school organization and
system policies, for example, should be evaluated on the basis
of their impact on the teaching/learning process. We do not
start from scratch here. In higher education, Alexander Astin's
work, AAHE's various forums and initiatives, and the Harvard
Assessment Seminars provide a variety of directions for building institutional sphere standards (Banta and Associates,
1993). In K–12, recent work on how changes in school structure affect student achievement suggests further fruitful
research (Bryk, Lee, and Holland, 1993; Bryk and Driscoll,
1988; Lee and Croninger, 1996; Bryk, Lee, and Smith, 1993).
In the external sphere, work on teacher networks across institutions or concerning institutes such as at Yale–New Haven
indicates the potential such collaborative links can have in
enhancing teacher repertoires, confidence, and reflective practices. Clearly research on the nonschool activities of students
provides another contribution to understanding how educators
might focus their energies for greatest impact, and how parents
might be best advised (Carnegie Corporation of New York,
1992; Carnegie Council on Adolescent Development, 1989;
"The Class of 2000," 1994; Wright and Huston, 1995; Wright
and Carr, 1995; Grissmer, Kirby, and Berends, 1994; Steinberg,
1996). The need for greater school-community articulation, as
well as increased links among the varied educational institutions serving a single community, focused upon particular intellectual goals for sphere one, demands even greater attention.
(For historical references, see Lawrence, 1944.) Educational
research should contribute to a clearer public understanding of
the degree to which various public policy decisions affect consensus teaching/learning goals.

20. Learning from English School Inspection seems advisable; see, for example, Wilson (1996).
21. It is interesting to note, for example, that while states were raising graduation requirements throughout the 1980s, many schools responded to more local concerns. The most common changes reported at the high school level between 1983 and 1988 were stricter attendance policies, "pass to play" rules, and stricter conduct codes. See Policy Information Center (1990, pp. 10–11.)
22. There are a number of interesting efforts in this direction, some building consensus for indicators and others setting our common principles of practice. In addition to drafts of new accreditation standards, see, for example, *Community Colleges* (1994); Ewell and others (1994). See also the work of the Southern Regional Education Board (1991, 1992, 1995) and Jaeger and others (1995a, 1995b); Jaeger, Johnson, and Gorney (1995). For a number of states that have put into place or are putting into place various styles of "feedback" systems, see Flanagan (1992).
23. Recent studies from the Public Agenda Foundation provide some intriguing results; see, for example, Farkas (1992, 1993); Farkas and Johnson (1996); Johnson (1995); Harvey and Immerwahr (1995a, 1995b); Harvey and Associates (1995).
24. As the ETS report *Learning by Degrees* indicates, there is a great deal we do not know about academic performance in the U.S.; this has not often hindered prescriptions (Barton and Lapointe, 1994). As a critic of reform hype added recently, "We need to learn that mass advocacy should follow, not precede, the careful development and large-scale testing of techniques" (Pogrow, 1996).

References

American College Testing and College Entrance Examination Board. *Education Reform and College Admission—Toward a Partnership*. Iowa City/New York: American College Testing and College Entrance Examination Board, 1994.

Armajani, B. H., Heydinger, R., and Hutchinson, P. *A Model for the Reinvented Higher Education System: State Policy and College Learning.* Denver: Education Commission of the States, 1994.

Aslanian, C. B. *Adult Learning in America—Why and How Adults Go Back to School.* New York: The College Board, 1996.

Banta, T. W., and Associates. *Making a Difference: Outcomes of a Decade of Assessment in Higher Education.* San Francisco: Jossey-Bass, 1993.

Barton, P. E., and Lapointe, A. *Learning by Degrees: Indicators of Performance in Higher Education.* Princeton, N.J.: Policy Information Center, Educational Testing Service, 1994.

Bond, L., with Friedman, L., and van der Ploog, A. *Surveying the Landscape of State Educational Assessment Programs.* Washington, D.C.: Council for Educational Development and Research, National Education Association, 1994.

Bond, L. A., and Roeber, E. D. *The Status of State Student Assessment Programs in the United States.* Annual Report. Washington, D.C.: Council of Chief State School Officers, 1995.

Bruer, J. T. "The Mind's Journey from Novice to Expert: If We Know the Route, We Can Help Students Negotiate Their Way." *American Educator,* Summer 1993a.

Bruer, J. T. *Schools for Thought—A Science of Learning in the Classroom.* Cambridge, Mass.: MIT Press, 1993b.

Bryk, A. S., and Driscoll, M. E. *The High School as Community: Contextual Influences and Consequences for Students and Teachers.* Madison: National Center on Effective Secondary Schools, University of Wisconsin, 1988.

Bryk, A. S., Lee, V. E., and Holland, P. B. *Catholic Schools and the Common Good.* Cambridge, Mass.: Harvard University Press, 1993.

Bryk, A. S., Lee, V. E., and Smith, J. B. "The Organization of Effective Secondary Schools." *Review of Research in Education,* 1993, *19,* 171–268.

Carnegie Corporation of New York. *A Matter of Time: Risk and Opportunity in the Nonschool Hours.* New York: Carnegie Corporation of New York, 1992.

Carnegie Council on Adolescent Development. *Turning Points: Preparing American Youth for the 21st Century.* New York: Carnegie Corporation of New York, 1989.

Carriuolo, N. *School-College Collaboration: A Way of Redesigning the Educational Pipeline.* Columbia: University of South Carolina, 1995.

"The Class of 2000." *ETS Policy Notes,* Fall 1994, *6,* 1.

Clune, W. H. *The Implementation and Effects of High School Graduation Requirements: First Steps Toward Curricular Reform.* RR-011. Madison, Wis.: Consortium for Policy Research in Education, 1989.

Clune, W. H., and White, P. A. "Education Reform in the Trenches: Increased Academic Course Taking in High Schools with Lower Achieving Students in States with Higher Graduation Requirements." *Educational Evaluation and Policy Analysis,* 1992, *14*(1), 2–20.

Clune, W. H., and others. *Changes in High School Course-Taking, 1982–88: A Study of Transcript Data from Selected Schools and States.* Madison, Wis.: Consortium for Policy Research in Education, 1991.

Cohen, D. K., and Spillane, J. P. "Policy and Practice: The Relations Between Governance and Instruction." *Review of Research in Education,* 1992, *18.*

Community Colleges: Core Indicators of Effectiveness. A report of the Community College Roundtable. Washington, D.C.: American Association of Community and Junior Colleges, 1994.

Cremin, L. A. *Traditions of American Education.* New York: Basic Books, 1976.

Cremin, L. A. *American Education: The Metropolitan Experience, 1876–1980.* New York: HarperCollins, 1988.

Cuban, L. "The Lure of Curricular Reform and Its Pitiful History." *Phi Delta Kappan,* Oct. 1993.

Darling-Hammond, L. "Reframing the School Reform Agenda: Developing the Capacity for School Transformation." *Phi Delta Kappan,* 1993, *74*(10), 752–761.

Dewey, J. *The School and Society.* Chicago: University of Chicago Press, 1899.

Dolan, W. P. *Restructuring Our Schools—A Primer on Systemic Change.* Kansas City, Mo.: Systems and Organization, 1994.

Druckman, D., and Bjork, R. A. (eds.). *Learning, Remembering, Believing.* Washington, D.C.: National Academy Press, 1994.

Dworkin, M. S. *Dewey on Education—Selections.* New York: Teachers College Press, 1959.

Eisner, E. W. "Educational Reform and the Ecology of Schooling." *Teachers College Record,* 1992, *93*(4), 610–627.

Eisner, E. W. "Do American Schools Need Standards?" *School Administrator,* May 1994, pp. 8–15.

Elmore, R. F. "Getting to Scale with Good Educational Practice." *Harvard Educational Review,* 1996, *66*(1), 1–26.

Elmore, R. F., and Fuhrman, S. H. *The Governance of Curriculum, 1994.* (Yearbook.) Alexandria, Va.: Association for Supervision and Curriculum Development, 1994.

Eurich, N. P. *The Learning Industry—Education for Adult Workers.* Princeton, N.J.: Carnegie Foundation for the Advancement of Teaching, 1990.

Ewell, P. T., and others. *A Preliminary Study of the Feasibility and Utility for National Policy of Instructional "Good Practice" Indicators in Undergraduate Education.* Washington, D.C.: National Center for Education Statistics, U.S. Department of Education, 1994.

Farkas, S. *Educational Reform: The Players and the Politics.* Charles Kettering Foundation Report. New York: Public Agenda Foundation, 1992.

Farkas, S. *Divided Within, Besieged Without: The Politics of Education in Four American School Districts.* New York: Public Agenda Foundation, 1993.

Farkas, S., and Johnson, J. *Given the Circumstances: Teachers Talk About Public Education Today.* New York: Public Agenda Foundation, 1996.

Fitzsimmons, P., and Peters, M. "Human Capital Theory and the Industry Training Strategy in New Zealand." *Journal of Education Policy,* 1994, 9(3), 245–266.

Flanagan, P. A. *Raising Standards: State Policies to Improve Academic Preparation for College.* Washington, D.C.: Office of Policy and Planning, U.S. Department of Education, 1992.

Fuhrman, S. H. (ed.). *Designing Coherent Education Policy: Improving the System.* San Francisco: Jossey-Bass, 1993.

Gagnon, P. A. *Seamless Subjects, Seamless Reform: Learning and Teaching Together, from Pre-School to Ph.D.* Occasional Paper. Westlake, Ohio: National Council for History Education, 1993.

Gardner, H. *Frames of Mind.* New York: Basic Books, 1981.

Gardner, H., and Boix-Mansilla, V. "Teaching for Understanding in the Disciplines—and Beyond." *Teachers College Record,* 1994, 96(2).

Grissmer, W., Kirby, S. N., and Berends, M. *Student Achievement and the Changing American Family.* Santa Monica, Calif.: RAND, Institute on Education and Training, 1994.

Harvey, J., and Associates. *First Impressions and Second Thoughts: Public Support for Higher Education.* Washington, D.C.: American Council on Education, 1995.

Harvey, J., and Immerwahr, J. *The Fragile Coalition: Public Support for Higher Education in the 1990s.* Washington, D.C.: American Council on Education, 1995a.

Harvey, J., and Immerwahr, J. *Goodwill and Growing Worry: Public Perceptions of American Higher Education.* Washington, D.C.: American Council on Education, 1995b.

Haycock, K. "Higher Education and the Schools: A Call to Action and Strategy for Change." *Metropolitan Universities,* Fall 1994, pp. 17–23.

Jaeger, R. M., Gorney, B., Johnson, R. L., Putnam, S. E., and Williamson, G. A *Consumer Report on School Report Cards.* Kalamazoo, Mich.: The Evaluation Center, Center for Research on Educational Accountability and Teacher Evaluation, 1995a.

Jaeger, R. M., Gorney, B., Johnson, R. L., Putnam, S. E., and Williamson, G. *Designing and Developing Effective Report Cards: A Research Synthesis.* Kalamazoo, Mich.: The Evaluation Center, Center for Research on Educational Accountability and Teacher Evaluation, 1995b.

Jaeger, R. M., Johnson, R. L., and Gorney, B. *The Nation's Schools Report to the Public: An Analysis of School Report Cards.* Kalamazoo, Mich.: The Evaluation Center, Center for Research on Educational Accountability and Teacher Evaluation, 1995.

Johnson, J. *Assignment Incomplete: The Unfinished Business of Education Reform.* New York: Public Agenda Foundation, 1995.

Kaestle, C. F. (ed.). *Joseph Lancaster and the Monitorial School Movement; A Documentary History.* New York: Teachers College Press, 1973.

Klein, S. *The Reliability of Mathematics Portfolio Scores: Lessons from the Vermont Experience.* Santa Monica, Calif.: RAND, 1994.

Koretz, D. S., Stecher, B., Klein, S., and McCaffrey, D. "The Vermont Portfolio Assessment Program: Findings and Implications." *Educational Measurement: Issues and Practice,* 1994, *13*(3).

Koretz, D., Stecher, B., and Debert, E. *The Vermont Portfolio Assessment Program: Interim Report on Implementation and Impact/1991–1992 School Year.* CSE Technical Report No. 350. Los Angeles: National Center for Research on Evaluation, Standards and Student Testing, 1992.

Koretz, D., Stecher, B., Klein, S., McCaffrey, D., and Debert, E. *Can Portfolios Assess Student Performance and Influence Instruction? The 1991–92 Vermont Experience.* RAND/RP-259. Santa Monica, Calif.: RAND, 1994.

Lagemann, E. C. "Experimenting with Education: John Dewey and Ella Flagg Young at the University of Chicago." *American Journal of Education,* May 1996, *104*, 171–185.

Lara, J. F., and Mitchell, R. "The Seamless Web—The Interdependence of Educational Institutions." *Education and Urban Society,* 1986, *19*(1), 24–41.

Lawrence, A. S. "American Schools Face the Minority Problem." *The New Era in Home and School,* 1944, *25*(6), 115–117.

Lawrence, L. *Profile of 1994–95 State Assessment Systems and Reported Results.* 96–05. Washington, D.C.: National Education Goals Panel, 1996.

Lazerson, M. *American Education in the Twentieth Century—A Documentary History.* Vol. 52. New York: Teachers College Press, 1987.

Lee, V. E., and Croninger, R. G. *Restructuring High Schools Can Improve Student Achievement.* Washington, D.C.: Center of Organizational Restructuring, 1996.

Lee, V. E., Smith, J. B., and Croninger, R. G. *Restructuring High Schools Can Improve Student Achievement.* Madison: University of Wisconsin, 1995.

Linn, R. L. "The Education Reform Agenda—Assessment, Standards, and the SAT." *College Board Review,* 1994, no. 172, 22–25, 30.

Little, J. W. "Teachers' Professional Development in a Climate of Educational Reform." In R. J. Anson (ed.), *Systemic Reform—Perspectives on Personalizing Education.* Washington, D.C.: Office of Educational Research and Improvement, U.S. Department of Education, 1994.

Lynd, R. S., and Lynd, H. M. *Middletown: A Study in American Culture.* New York: Harcourt, Brace & Co, 1929.

Massell, D. F., Fuhrman, S., and Associates. *Ten Years of State Education Reform, 1983–1993: Overview with Four Case Studies.* RR-028. Madison, Wis.: Consortium for Policy Research in Education, 1994.

McLoughlin, W. G. *Revivals, Awakenings, and Reform—An Essay on Religion and Social Change in America, 1607–1977.* Chicago: University of Chicago Press, 1978.

Mitchell, R. "Measuring Up: Student Assessment and Systemic Change." *Educational Technology,* 1992, *32*, 37–41.

Moyers, B. A *World of Ideas—Conversations with Thoughtful Men and Women About American Life Today and the Ideas Shaping Our Future*. New York: Doubleday, 1989.

Newman, M. "Cortines Hails Effort to Push Tough Classes." *New York Times*, May 9, 1995, pp. B1, B4.

Newmann, F. M. "School-wide Professional Community." *Issues in Restructuring Schools*, Spring 1994, no. 6.

Newmann, F. M., and Wehlage, G. G. *Successful School Restructuring*. Madison, Wis.: Center on Organization and Restructuring of Schools, 1995.

Noble, A. J., and Smith, M. L. *Measurement-Driven Reform: The More Things Change, the More They Stay the Same*. CRESST/CSE Technical Report 373. Los Angeles: National Center for Research on Evaluation, Standards and Student Testing, 1994a.

Noble, A. J., and Smith, M. L. "Old and New Beliefs About Measurement-Driven Reform: 'Build It and They Will Come.'" *Educational Policy*, 1994b, 8(2), 111–136.

O'Day, J., Goertz, M. E., and Floden, R. E. *Building Capacity for Education Reform*. (Policy Brief.) Madison, Wis.: Consortium for Policy Research in Education, 1995.

Perkins, D. *Smart Schools: From Training Memories to Educating Minds*. New York: Free Press, 1992.

Peters, R. "Some Snarks are Boojums: Accountability and the End(s) of Higher Education." *Change*, Nov./Dec. 1994.

Pogrow, S. "Reforming the Wannabe Reformers." *Phi Delta Kappan*, June 1996, p. 11.

Policy Information Center. *The Education Reform Decade*. Princeton, N.J.: Educational Testing Service, 1990.

Porter, A. C. *Standard Setting and the Reform of High School Mathematics and Science*: Madison: University of Wisconsin, 1995.

Porter, A. C., and Associates. *Reform of High School Mathematics and Science and Opportunity to Learn*. Policy Brief RB–13. Madison, Wis.: Consortium for Policy Research in Education, 1994.

Presidential Task Force on Psychology in Education, American Psychological Association. *Learner-Centered Psychological Principles: Guidelines for School Redesign and Reform*. Washington, D.C.: American Psychological Association and the Mid-Continent Regional Educational Laboratory, Jan. 1993.

"Reforming Science, Mathematics, and Technology Education: NSF's State Systemic Initiatives." Policy Brief RB-15-May. Madison, Wis.: Consortium for Policy Research in Education, 1995.

Reigart, J. F. *The Lancasterian System of Instruction in the Schools of New York City*. New York: Arno Press, 1969.

Scheffler, I. "In Praise of the Cognitive Emotions." In *In Praise of the Cognitive Emotions*. New York: Routledge, 1991.

Shepard, L. A., and Bleim, C. L. *An Analysis of Parent Opinions and Changes in Opinions Regarding Standardized Tests, Teacher Information, and Performance Assessments.* CSE Technical Report 397. Los Angeles: National Center for Research on Evaluation, Standards and Student Testing/University of Colorado at Boulder, 1995.

Shepard, L. A., and others. *Effects of Introducing Classroom Performance Assessments on Student Learning.* CSE Technical Report 394. Los Angeles: National Center for Research on Evaluation, Standards and Student Testing/University of Colorado at Boulder, 1995.

Smith, M. S., and O'Day, J. "Systemic School Reform." *Politics of Education Association Yearbook, 1990.* London: Taylor & Francis, 1990.

Southern Regional Education Board. *Report Cards for Education: Accountability in SREB States.* Atlanta: Southern Regional Education Board, 1991.

Southern Regional Education Board. *School Accountability Reports: Lessons Learned in SREB States.* Atlanta: Southern Regional Education Board, 1992.

Southern Regional Education Board. *Linking Education Report Cards and Local School Improvement.* Atlanta: Southern Regional Education Board, 1995.

Speaker's Blue Ribbon Commission on Career/Technical Education. *Redefining the Purpose of Education: Providing Students with a Seamless Transition from School-to-Work.* Lansing: Michigan State Legislature, 1992.

State University of New York, Task Force on College Entry-Level Knowledge and Skills. *College Expectations: Knowledge and Skills.* Albany: State University of New York, 1995.

Stecklow, S. "Virtual U at Phoenix University: Class Can Be Anywhere—Even in Cyberspace." *Wall Street Journal,* Sept. 12, 1994, p. 3.

Steinberg, L. *Beyond the Classroom—Why School Reform Has Failed and What Parents Need to Do.* New York: Simon & Schuster, 1996.

Stewart, D. M. "The College Board: Lessons from Two Decades of School-College Collaboration." In N. Carriuolo, *School-College Collaboration: A Way of Redesigning the Educational Pipeline.* Columbia: University of South Carolina, 1995.

Tyack, D. B. *The One Best System: A History of American Urban Education.* Cambridge, Mass.: Harvard University Press, 1974.

Tyack, D. "Reinventing Schooling." In D. Ravitch and M. Vinovskis (eds.), *Learning from the Past—What History Teaches Us About School Reform.* Baltimore: Johns Hopkins University Press, 1995.

Valentine, J. A. *The College Board and the School Curriculum.* New York: College Board, 1987.

Wang, M. C., Haertel, G. D., and Walberg, H. J. "What Influences Learning? A Content Analysis of Review Literature." *Journal of Educational Research,* 1990, *84*(1).

Wang, M. C., Haertel, G. D., and Walberg, H. J. "Effective Practices and Poli-
    cies: Research and Practitioner Views." Paper presented at the annual
    meeting of the American Educational Research Association, San Fran-
    cisco, 1995.

Wiggins, G. *Toward One System of Education: Assessing to Improve, Not Merely
    Audit*. Denver: Center on Learning, Assessment and School Structure,
    1991.

Wilson, T. A. *Reaching for a Better Standard: English School Inspection and the
    Dilemma of Accountability for American Public Schools*. New York: Teach-
    ers College Press, 1996.

Wright, J. C., and Huston, A. C. *Effects of Educational TV Viewing of Lower
    Income Preschoolers on Academic Skills, School Readiness, and School
    Adjustment One to Three Years Later*. Lawrence: Center for Research on
    the Influences of Television on Children, University of Kansas, 1995.

Wright, J. D., and Carr, R. *Effects of High School Work Experience a Decade Later*.
    Washington, D.C.: Employment Policies Institute Foundation, 1995.

Chapter Eight

Higher Education and the Schools

An Alien Commentary

Harry Judge

The American Exception?

This chapter takes the form of an essay written by a friendly and fascinated foreigner around the themes that recur throughout the pages of this collaborative book. Its central argument is that within the covers of this volume is deployed yet one more example of American exceptionality. Why is it that no other nation appears to be so preoccupied with the issue defined as central to the whole of this book? Why do few, if any, other countries give serious attention to what in the United States appears to be highly problematic: namely, the relationship of higher education to the public school system and the role of the former in the reform of the latter (or indeed vice versa)?

There are especially good reasons for bringing a comparative perspective to bear on these questions. The most obvious of these is that the American system (or nonsystem) is in itself so vast that for those working within it there is a perpetual temptation never to look beyond its own dauntingly wide frontiers. This, indeed, is true of many aspects of U.S. policy: the economy most notably, political organization, health, law and order, defense. The temptation is

---

This essay is based largely on the arguments of the other chapters in this book and on interviews extending over a number of years in the United States, France, and England.

especially magnetic in education, where there prevails within the fifty states a bewildering diversity of practice and belief, a unique range of institutional patterns (especially within higher education itself), a variety of public policies (varying, that is to say, from state to state). Few students of education have therefore either the time or the motivation to look seriously at foreign comparisons or contrasts. This chapter consciously eschews any naive suggestion that there are any simple "lessons" to be learned from foreign "examples," but it does assert that the study of some foreign situations will throw new light on American preoccupations, and perhaps (at least indirectly) assist in the resolution of some problems, old and new.

This is the kind of comparison that will therefore be attempted in these pages. It is in no sense a matter of plucking out specific and encouraging examples of what might appear to be good practice in exotic places: for example, the engagement of senior university personnel in the academic life of high schools; the influence of universities on the evaluation and examination of students in schools; the overlap in teachers' careers between secondary and higher education; or the building of partnerships between regional and central government with local enterprises in the field of vocational education. All these things do happen "elsewhere"; but they happen for precise and local reasons, and cannot be magically transplanted. The purpose here is rather to stress that all national education systems consist of distinctive connections of interlocking parts, and to show by contrasts why U.S. concerns are as they are.

The contrasting examples that appear in the following pages are those of England (which is not Scotland) and France. Each of the two nations is sufficiently different from the other, as well as sufficiently different from the United States, to allow some key points to emerge with sharp clarity. The English system is one that has for long given great weight to national needs and centralized planning, balanced by a healthy respect for the preferences of local democracy and a belief in the devolution of authority to professionals, including those working in the schools. That system is, of course, at the moment accelerating rapidly toward a privatized and market-oriented pattern of provision in both schools and higher education, but even that shift is itself a result of government propulsion rather than of spontaneous change. The English system has also, throughout its evolution, been deeply marked (as for example in the Advanced Level examinations taken by high school graduates) by an academic or university-type set of curricular preoccupations within the high schools. These preoccupations persist, albeit in growing tension with the imperatives of mass secondary education and with a remarkable widening of access to higher education itself.

The French system, on the other hand, has always been represented (not always accurately or fairly) as a highly centralized top-down set of arrangements, with a national curriculum and tightly managed machinery of inspection for teachers and schools. Even more plainly than the English system, it is dominated by an academic intellectualism, well typified by the recognition of the graduation diploma as the first university degree (the *baccalauréat*, that is), by the formal direction of the whole educational system (including the very well-developed preschool sector), by university scholars (the rectors presiding over the academies), and by a complex overlap of higher education and the schools across that powerful sector of education concerned with preparation for competitive entry to the *Grandes Écoles*. This historic interpenetration of higher and school education generates a wholly distinctive educational and administrative culture. Indeed, at one time the high schools were themselves the very core of the University of France. In spite of fundamental changes over the past fifteen years—involving both a high degree of decentralization from Paris and a growing democratization in access to the *baccalauréat*—these traditional bases of the French system remain firm and solid.

The Context of School Reform in America

The chapters forming the body of this volume represent a contribution to the growing literature of "School Reform" (with capital letters selected deliberately). School reform of course is and has been a recurring theme in the educational debates of most countries—including France and England—although perhaps never to the extent marked by the feverish concerns of the 1980s and 1990s. Although subtle and important distinctions among European countries must be borne in mind, reform has been generally perceived as the unavoidable and perennial responsibility of a national government. Although particular politicians—say, Lionel Jospin in France or Kenneth Baker in England—may attempt to capture the glamour of a dramatic moment in reform, it is widely taken for granted both that the reforming process is continuous (even indistinguishable from the routine management of the system) and that its propulsion is the proper if not exclusive business of the government of the day. It is never going to be "done" ("achieved," that is), and it is propelled by government initiative rather than by a dispersed public movement.

These things are obviously not so in the United States. Rather, there is across the continent a broad public presumption that School Reform is something to be achieved by a "Movement," that all those seeking to change schools (however diverse their objectives and distinct their methods) somehow constitute a part of the same enterprise, that they are all moving in the same direction and that Reform will be achieved by a generous mixture of tactics at every level of power and influence. Presidents may exhort from the bully pulpit while secretaries of education suggest what needs to be done, Congress may (however grudgingly) approve the notion of national goals while leaving to States and communities the establishment of specific standards, governors and legislators will change regulations and redirect funding, school boards will rethink their policies, business leaders will bring their skills and resources to the common and patriotic task, building administrators will reconceptualize their roles, teachers will collaborate and be empowered, charitable foundations will be mobilized to provide financial support for a whole stable of projects, national bodies of scholars and educators will develop elaborate standards for teachers and for the curriculum in each subject, teacher education and professional development will be reshaped, communities will reconnect to their schools, apostolic reformers will build coalitions and inspire education with new ideas and fresh ideals. . . . This heady mixture is distilled as the antidote to the alleged sickness of U.S. education, which by its failures weakens national competitiveness and fails to serve those very students who need and deserve most from schooling.

There are no international examples to place alongside such an overarching concept of a School Reform Movement. A comparative profile of U.S. School Reform brings out clearly some of its distinctive characteristics, related to many of the long continuities of American culture. There is in all this more than a whiff of evangelistic individualism, a belief that private and voluntary (not government) effort can bring salvation and cure many temporal ills. There is a strong flavor of optimism and of competitiveness, of the will to succeed, as well as of a deeply human concern with the less advantaged, who should be helped to save themselves by their own efforts. This deep conviction that if only enough were done the problem would be "fixed," and education would once and for all be okay, is rooted in a reluctance to admit that educational reform might after all be more like the endless and uninspiring work of weeding a luxuriant and undisciplined garden.

These remarks, be assured, carry no hint of a decadent Old World disdain for the irrepressible enthusiasm of the New. On the contrary. Many living outside the United States have good reason to envy the width of public interest and support massed behind the banners of the Education Reform Movement. But in recent years a new, and in some ways puzzling, element has been injected into the language of Reform. "Systemic reform," not always defined clearly or in a uniform manner, is now projected as the latest, if not the last, answer to the apparent intractability of a huge and (it is alleged) seriously malfunctioning educational enterprise. The darker side of the eschatological optimism of much U.S. educational Reform language —all will be well if only the right prescription can be found and zealously applied (progressivism, scientific management, child-centeredness, constructivism, back to basics, programmed learning, team teaching, technology, devolution, school site management . . .)—has in the past often led in short order to an equally exaggerated pessimism. As an antiphon to "everything is possible," the plangent refrain closing every stanza in a long story of attempts to fix "the" problem recurs as "nothing has worked."

This perpetual failure is now explained on the grounds that attempts to reform have in the past attacked the parts (curriculum, teacher preparation, finance, team teaching, assessment) without tackling the whole, without recognizing that all the parts of the problem, and therefore of any solution to it, are interrelated in a pattern of complex causality. The whole is logically antecedent to the parts. In a society that has traditionally prided itself on being pluralist and nonsystemic, this novel stress upon "system" strikes the foreign observer as paradoxically odd. It is, of course, axiomatic that in a system like the French, all reform has in principle to be patterned and orderly, because that is simply how things are and are meant to be.

Higher Education and the Schools: Contrasting Systems

Why then have Americans, and Americans alone, cast in a particular way the "problem" of the relationships between higher education and the schools? In those European systems which work in reasonably predictable ways, the problem (if there is one) is a problem for government and the pressure groups that seek directly to influence national policy. It is not essentially a question of local agreement and cooperation, or of remedying the deficiencies in such collaborations. It is the business of government, in France and England as in so many countries, to manage the flow of students from schools to higher education and of school teachers from universities back into the schools. It is the business of government to align the curricula of schools (often through a national examination for high school graduates) with the expectations of universities receiving those students a few months later—and European higher education is for the great majority of students still a direct sequel to the school experience. It is the business of government, with minimal supplementary assistance from other sources, to provide the resources needed to support both the public and national school system and the public and national university system: Private institutions of higher education have only a peripheral part to play on the national scenes. Of course, whether governments do these things well or ill is quite another matter. In the United States, on the other hand, once the obvious appeal of the systemic argument is acknowledged, the business of making the system work better (since there is and could be no supreme national coordination of efforts) has to be undertaken by the participants themselves. The parts have to make the whole, and make it work.

Hence the special flavor of much of the discussion in this book. That flavor is further enriched by the (again, in international terms, unusual) character of higher education in the United States. Only in some unhelpfully loose way can that higher education be described as forming an educational "sector," even in the sense in which the K–12 schools nationally constitute such an entity. Although neither the French nor the English systems of higher education is marked by a boring uniformity, each of them does have a consistency and coherence significantly absent from the United States.

The French system is unusual in including a relatively small but highly prestigious group of *Grandes Écoles*, entry to which is highly competitive. The classes that prepare for admission to these elite establishments are often found within high schools (*Lycées*) and formally constitute part of higher rather than secondary education. The universities, as fundamentally reorganized after the troubles of 1968, now form a relatively homogeneous block of institutions: state funded, with faculty appointments made nationally, awarding government-accredited degrees and diplomas while for the most part serving regional needs. Most advanced research, especially in the natural sciences, is located in specially funded centers, nationally managed and often only loosely connected to universities. Each university, although less so than in the past, forms an integral part of the whole educational system, serving the needs of students from the age of three upward. That system is divided into a series of regional "academies," each under the supervision of the rector, himself a tenured university professor nominated to that respected position for a limited period by the minister of national education. It is as though, in the United States, a senior university professor were empowered by Washington for a discretionary period to assume the enlarged powers of a chief state school officer and a superintendent. Reporting to the rector and to the minister in Paris is a phalanx of inspectors, many of them seeing their place in the world as intellectual and academic rather than managerial. There is in such a universe no obvious "problem" either in defining or in nurturing a relationship between universities and schools. (Needless to say, there are plenty of other problems to worry about.)

There is greater variety—although not approaching American standards—within the English system. Within the past few years, the number of institutions designated as universities has doubled (by the inclusion of the former polytechnics), and all of them are funded by a common agency on a relatively equitable basis. There is a wider range of reputation and quality among English than French universities (since the *Grandes Écoles* themselves are not universities): All but one of them are public and not private. Universities award their own degrees, albeit within a policy framework that attempts to establish a reasonable measure of comparability.

The English example (itself rapidly changing and becoming more competitive and "American") stands between the French and the U.S. examples, with the latter embracing a uniquely wide and relatively uncoordinated range of institutions, missions, and reputations. Many of these institutions are private and are found at every level of a complex system; most, of course, are public. Some establishments are two-year colleges, often serving purely local needs. At the peak of a hierarchical yet flexible pyramid stand the universities (both private and public) of high international esteem, richly endowed with graduate schools and esteemed for their research in many or all of the established disciplines. States can and do apply policies, sometimes rigorously, to the universities and colleges within their jurisdiction and financially dependent on them, but such control ceases at each state border and rarely affects private institutions. Universities need to compete for resources at the national level, and each institution is obliged to create its own niche in a luxuriant system.

We are now at the heart of the dilemma that lurks behind many of the chapters in this volume. If reform is to be effective it must be systemic. If it is to be systemic, there must be no seams between school and higher education. Yet higher education never constitutes (even to the extent that it does in countries such as England) any kind of unity. Within it institutions must find their own place and status and are often obliged to compete with one another. Nobody may be allowed to define for them their assigned place in the world. Establishing such a place requires a great deal of concentration and specialization, and in the absence of any structured links there is often no reason for higher education to concern itself with K–12 schooling, which might best be left to its own devices.

There are therefore powerful reasons for those living in academe to avert their eyes from the problems of schools. But university presidents and others with responsibilities for institutional health cannot afford to take so narrow a view. There is an American "problem" because many, if by no means all, public universities are—whether they like it or not—part of a local as well as a national network, and compete for attention and resources with many other suitors, inside as well as outside the educational ranks. Public, and to a lesser extent private, universities cannot flourish without generous subsidy and visible support from the local political community—from, that is to say, governors and state legislators and, behind them, the members of the public upon whose votes they depend. A university that shows little or no concern for the welfare of the public schools and little willingness to participate in their reform will soon lose support from public sources. There is no real parallel to this situation in most other developed countries, and certainly not in France or England. In both those countries, and in England even more obviously since the removal of the former polytechnics from local control, funding depends almost entirely on national sources and there is much less local interest in and pressure on institutions of higher education to behave as responsible and responsive local citizens. There may, of course, be reasons derived from enlightened principle for universities in the United States to busy themselves with local problems, and in particular with education in the public schools; there are certainly overwhelming reasons suggested by prudence.

The reasons for the exceptional U.S. concern with the relationships between schools and higher education may now be drawn together. Although the United States is painfully conscious of having a national education and a national educational problem (what else could explain either the title or the contents of *A Nation at Risk?*), this "national" education may not constitute a system, in the senses in which Europeans understand that term. A national "system" is not at all the same thing as a federal system. If reform, or more revealingly Reform, is at last to be achieved, then it must be by the widest possible form of consensus and coalition. The motives and objectives of those who voluntarily come together in a determination to "fix" the problem are diverse and need not be examined too closely. They all want change. This open coalition constitutes the Education Reform Movement, which is of course not a movement in any conventional sense. The exceptional optimism of the American spirit is counterbalanced by cyclical bursts of a pessimism that seems never to prove fatal. "Nothing has worked but something now will." Reform, since by definition it requires collaboration, must plainly engage higher as well as school education in some kind of joint enterprise. In this there is nothing new, although universities have often wavered in the enthusiasm of their commitment to a deep engagement with schools. They have competitive interests of their own to protect. Nevertheless, the pressure for them to engage in the language and even the hard practice of reform is now heightened by two factors: the dependence of higher education on public support and funding, made more vulnerable by widespread criticisms; and the relatively recent emphasis upon systemic reform, the broad principles of which it is difficult to controvert. If Reform has failed simply because it has not been systemic, then its success requires that all parts of the system (if the word may be used in an ecological rather than mechanistic sense) must be engaged in interlocking and simultaneous effort.

Higher Education and the Schools: Contrasting Connections

There is in the United States a cultural gap of intimidating width and depth between the two worlds of school and higher education. Gaps in other countries tend to be cracks rather than chasms. It is a historical truism, but a useful one, that in the United States the high school grew—with the well-known exceptions such as Boston Latin—from the stock of the common (elementary) school, and was never dominated by the colleges or the universities. In much of Europe, on the other hand, the elite secondary school was—in some cases literally, and in most figuratively—a colony established in pagan territory by the missionary university. In England symbols were important in driving home this distinction. In nearly all the selective grammar schools, which until recently covered the country, as in most of the private secondary schools, the teachers—dignified with the title of Master or Mistress—wore university robes as they went about their daily teaching. The Advanced Level examinations, like those of similar character that preceded them, were originally designed, promoted, and administered by the universities, which to this day remain dominant in the setting of standards at this influential level.

The movement to create comprehensive high schools (approved or despised in the 1960s and 1970s as American in origin and inspiration) weakened but never destroyed these intimate and subtle connections. That movement is in any case now being subjected to severe challenges: the Labor Government that came to power in May 1997 proved to be as determined as its Conservative predecessor to protect high academic standards, traditionally defined. Politics and polemics apart, teachers of history or mathematics in English secondary schools of all kinds see themselves (and are generally perceived) as belonging to the same professional academic caste as their university colleagues. In England, but surely not in America, such teachers can describe themselves (with no hint of presumptuous arrogance) as "mathematicians" or "historians." All this suggests that whereas in England a fault line runs between primary and secondary education, in the United States an even clearer line falls between the schools and higher education.

The French system presents stark contrasts of a different sort. Although the dividing lines (for example in teacher education, discussed below) are less sharp than they once were, no one even today could confuse the culture of the primary school with that of the *Lycée*, insulated from one another as they are by the neutral zone of the middle school. The power of the university-based rector and the organization of all public education through regional Academies, the *baccalauréat* as both high school graduation and national university degree, the substantial presence within *Lycée* buildings of a good deal of formal higher education of the highest quality, the stress on academic content in the recruitment of secondary teachers, the use of the title of professor for those teachers: All these are at once causes and symptoms of the intimate alliance between the schools, and especially the higher secondary schools, and the university. The absence in the United States of natural lines of communication of this order explain much of the uneasiness of the relationship across the great divide. In the United States then, but not in Europe, it seems natural to talk of K–12 as a seamless continuum having little in common with a higher education that is its sequel. In Europe, the contrasts between primary (or elementary) and secondary schooling are at least as strong, if not stronger, than those between secondary and higher education.

Nothing illuminates more clearly the exceptionality of U.S. formulations of the problem of higher education–school relationships than the way in which the three countries manage the business of teacher education in the context of higher education. After all, one of the most obvious pieces of traffic across the frontier is made up of the teachers educated in universities and then returning to teach in the schools. It is not the case that the relationship is unproblematic in any of the countries—far from it—but it is problematic in significantly different ways. Most countries share long histories of distrust and suspicion in the world of teacher education, where higher education and the schools meet and sometimes collide. Those who work in and for schools often accuse the universities of neglecting the real needs of future teachers, of engaging in much ethereal or irrelevant theory, of not respecting the skills and wisdom that experienced teachers can bring to the formation of a profession. Academics, and especially those in Schools and Departments of Education (where such entities exist), are for their part convinced that the schools are unappreciative of what educational theory can contribute to the effectiveness of teaching, as also of what universities can do to instill in teachers those qualities of critical independence that are the hallmark of a profession.

Earlier in this century, the prevailing English conviction was that secondary teachers needed little more than a good grounding in the discipline that they were going to teach. Such formal training as the universities provided remained for many years optional and was treated as peripheral. Teachers of younger students received a different form of preparation in single-purpose colleges, combining the rudiments of a general education with a good deal of pedagogy. In the second half of this century the universities became more involved in all teacher education, but in the process attracted to themselves many of the general criticisms identified above. Government, with public acquiescence if not support, has now intervened powerfully by taking from the universities the kind of autonomy in the provision of teacher education that they had long taken for granted. Criteria for the necessary official approval of their education programs have since 1980 consistently stressed the importance (indeed the priority) of practical experience in schools under the supervision of experienced teachers. The funding of teacher training has been removed from the general budget for universities and is now separately administered in accordance with government priorities. A national curriculum for teachers is now being introduced. Within a highly systemic context, government authority has therefore been used to redefine the frontier between higher education and the schools, and to diminish the importance of whatever it is that universities, as distinctive institutions, might contribute to the intellectual and professional lives of teachers in schools of all kinds. The "problem" has been dealt with.

The French experience has been predictably different. The classical normal schools of the nineteenth century, albeit in an attenuated form, survived right into the last decade of the twentieth century. They had been created to produce a supply of well-prepared teachers for the primary schools of the Republic: Before the 1980s they were not even recognized as part of higher education. Their direction was closely associated with the government inspectorate, and practice schools were often linked with them. They were an integral part of (and not a neighbor of) primary education. In the 1970s uncertain steps were taken to build connections to the universities, but none led to any significant changes.

The training of secondary school teachers proceeded from quite different assumptions. The first part of their program (taken after completing a normal period of general higher education) was and remains strongly academic in emphasis. It concludes with a rigorously competitive examination, giving admission to a salaried status and a year of preparation for the practical and professional tasks of teaching. Until the recent reform, responsibility for that preparation belonged exclusively to the school inspectorate, working in a variety of institutional settings. Unlike England, France did not suffer from the existence of a no-man's-land between the separate territories occupied by higher education and by the schools.

Much in France has been changed by the reforms of the 1990s, and all teacher training—primary as well as secondary—is now conducted by newly constituted university institutes. But in France the frontier between higher education and the schools is more peaceful and planned than in either England or America. The French solution to the management of the frontier has been to preserve the active participation of school personnel (inspectors and others) in the training of teachers, to bring that work into an administrative framework clearly defined at the national level and administered regionally by the rectors, and to persist in assigning to the main body of the university (perceived as a federation of subject departments) an equally clear responsibility for the subject-matter education of all future teachers. Little or no attention is paid within the university itself either to pedagogy or to what in the United States have come to be described as educational foundations—the philosophy and history of education, child development and psychology, sociology. A distinctive partnership of teachers in schools with university academics has been defined by Paris. Within a highly systemic context the "problem" has been dealt with.

In these two European countries the management of the frontier between schools and higher education, and the critically important sector of teacher education, has therefore in the past five years been approached in strikingly different ways: One increases traffic across that frontier, while the other severely restricts it. But in both countries the solutions have been quite plainly systemic and therefore related to a whole series of other items on the agenda of educational reform (revaluing teaching, defining higher standards, increasing accountability, establishing national norms, checking the autonomy of higher education), and in both cases the changes have been imposed by government.

Once again, the exceptionality of the U.S. situation asserts itself, for in the United States the critically important frontier turns out to be more like a zone than a line. Relationships are untidy, unmanaged, often uncomfortable, frequently negotiated locally on an ad hoc basis, shifting, varying from institution to institution.

202 HIGHER EDUCATION AND SCHOOL REFORM

This is not the place to rehearse the difficulties and dilemmas of teacher education in the States, but it may be useful to indicate some of the points at which those problems directly relate to the themes of this chapter and of this book.

Because ambitious universities prosper when their research achievements are visible and acknowledged, in an open market they are driven to value research above teaching and above service. Their critics in the schools, in the past even more than in the present, have interpreted this preference as proving that the most prestigious parts of higher education are not concerned with the perplexities of the public schools. Because school teaching (certainly compared with the French example) is not a highly regarded professional activity, university schools of education also tend to pay less attention to the needs of beginning teachers in the schools and more to serving the needs of upwardly mobile teachers aspiring to become administrators, counselors, or researchers: Again, the schools are left with a sense of loss or desertion. Because American secondary education has achieved levels of democratization undreamed of (until very recently) in other countries, its curriculum is of necessity open and generous, and the traditionally academic content diluted. Secondary has therefore more in common with elementary than with higher education, and communication between the latter two is impeded. Because there is no planning for the labor market in teaching and no obvious connection between the output (of new teachers) from higher education and the input to the schools, the relationships between the two are only loosely articulated. Because there are no national norms, the matching within higher education of the interests of the arts and science schools with those of the education schools can never be precise and explicit. In the European countries discussed here (and many other developed societies) there is indeed a clearer sense of which of the constituent parts of a university are related to the needs of the public schools, and how. These are among the problems that vigorous reform groups concerned centrally with teacher education have been attacking through the past decade.

All this means that Americans will need to go on worrying about the relationship between higher education and the schools, and addressing the key issues through specific reform efforts, through the building of coalitions, through attempts to influence those who make policy and apply it. There will be no "answer," the problem will not be solved, nothing will work, and everything will have to be done again, and again. That, as Americans consider some of the examples offered in this alien commentary, is not necessarily a crippling disadvantage. It is sometimes better to suffer a sore toe than to have a foot amputated.

Resources

Among the books published over the past decade and which the author has found useful are the following:

Auduc, J.-L. *Le système Éducatif*. Paris: Hachette, 1994.

Ball, S. J. *Politics and Policy Making in Education*. London: Routledge, 1990.

Berliner, D. C., and Biddle, B. J. *The Manufactured Crisis: Myths, Frauds and the Attack on America's Public Schools*. Reading, Mass.: Addison-Wesley, 1995.

Bridges, D. (ed). *Education in the Market Place*. London: Falmer, 1994.

Charlot, J. *La politique en France*. Paris: Livre de Poche, 1996.

Chubb, J. E., and Moe, T. E. *A Lesson in School Reform from Great Britain*. Washington, D.C.: Brookings Institution, 1992.

Clark, B. R. (ed.) *The School and the University: An International Perspective*. Berkeley: University of California Press, 1985.

Clifford, G. J., and Guthrie, J. W. *Ed School: A Brief for Professional Education*. Chicago: University of Chicago Press, 1988.

Elmore, R. F., and McLaughlin, M. *Steady Work: Policy, Practice and the Reform of American Education*. Santa Monica, Calif.: RAND Corporation, 1988.

Jenkins, S. *Accountable to None: The Tory Nationalization of the State*. London: Hamish Hamilton, 1995.

Judge, H., Lemosse, M., Paine, L., and Sedlak, M. *The University and the Teachers: France, the United States, England*. Wallingford, England: Triangle Books, 1994.

Lawton, D. *The Tory Mind on Education 1979–1994*. London: Falmer, 1994.

Lipset, S. M. *American Exceptionalism*. New York: Norton, 1988.

Maclure, S. *Education Re-Formed: A Guide to the Education Reform Act 1988*. London: Hodder and Stoughton, 1988.

Nique, C. *L'impossible gouvernement des esprits: l'histoire politique des Écoles normales primaires*. Paris: Nathan, 1991.

Powell, A. G., Farrar, E., and Cohen, D. *The Shopping Mall High School: Winners and Losers in the Educational Marketplace*. Boston: Houghton Mifflin, 1985.

Prost, A. *Education, société et politiques: une histoire de l'enseignement en France de 1945 à nos jours*. Paris: Seuil, 1992.

Rouet, G., and Savontchick, S. *Dictionnaire pratique de l'enseignement en France: de la maternelle au supérieur*. Paris: Ellipses, 1996.

Salter, B., and Tapper, T. *The State and Higher Education*. Woburn, England: Ilford Press, 1994.

Shattock, M. *The UGC and the Management of British Universities*. Buckingham, England: Open University Press, 1994.

Stearns, K. *School Reform: Lessons from England*. Princeton, N.J.: Carnegie Foundation for the Advancement of Teaching, 1996.

Toulemonde, B. *Petite histoire d'une grande ministère: l'Éducation Nationale*. Paris: Albin Michel, 1988.

Verger, J. (ed.) *Histoire des universités en France*. Toulouse, France: Privat, 1986.

Index